Latin America's Leaders

About the Authors

RUT DIAMINT is professor of international relations in the Department of Political Science and International Studies at Universidad Torcuato di Tella, researcher at the National Council for Scientific and Technological Research (CONICET) and a member of the Advisory Committee of Club de Madrid and the UN Secretary General Advisory Board on Disarmament Matters. She has been visiting professor at Columbia University, and has received scholarships from Fulbright, the Woodrow Wilson International Center for Scholars, the PIF programme of the Canadian government, the Tinker Foundation, the UN Commission for Peace Studies and the US Studies Center for US–Mexican Studies, University of California at San Diego.

LAURA TEDESCO is associate professor of political science at Saint Louis University, Madrid Campus, and at Instituto de Empresa, Madrid. She has received scholarships from the British Council, the Foreign and Commonwealth Office and CONICET (Argentina) and grants from the British Academy and the Open Society Institute. She has taught at Universidad de Buenos Aires, FLACSO, the University of Warwick and the University of East Anglia. She has been a consultant for UNICEF and worked as an analyst for FRIDE, Spain.

Latin America's Leaders

RUT DIAMINT AND LAURA TEDESCO

Zed Books | LONDON

Latin America's Leaders was first published in 2015 by Zed Books Ltd, The Foundry, 17 Oval Way, London SE11 5RR, UK.

www.zedbooks.co.uk

Typeset in Monotype Bulmer by Lumina Datamatics Ltd.
Index: John Barker
Cover designed by www.stevenmarsden.com

A catalogue record for this book is available from the British Library.

ISBN 978-1-78360-103-5 hb
ISBN 978-1-78360-102-8 pb
ISBN 978-1-78360-104-2 pdf
ISBN 978-1-78360-105-9 epub
ISBN 978-1-78360-106-6 mobi

MIX
Paper from
responsible sources
FSC® C013604

Printed and bound by CPI Group (UK) Ltd, Croydon, CR0 4YY

To Alex, Simona, Ema, Matilda, Luna and Rita

Contents

Figures and Tables

Acknowledgements

This book is the result of seven years of collaborative study. We began to debate the democratic quality of Latin American political leaders in 2008. In the beginning our discussions were part of informal meetings. Slowly we became more intrigued about political leaders in Latin America and a literature review started to take shape. We realized that the bibliography on political leadership in the region was very limited. Although political leaders have always been important in our region, academics have neglected their study, while internationally the bibliography about political leadership was growing. Thus, we established an agenda to discuss research questions on leadership, and at the beginning of 2009 started to work on a research proposal.

Our project was accepted by the Foundation of Open Society Institute (FOSI) in Washington, DC. We want to thank María Victoria Wigodsky, who shared our enthusiasm for and preoccupation over political leaders. FOSI gave us generous financial support for three years, which allowed us to conduct interviews in Buenos Aires, Bogotá, Caracas, Montevideo, Quito and Washington.

We were able to manage the project, prepare events and organize the interviews thanks to a fantastic team of collaborators in different

countries. Juan Pablo Ochoa (Quito); Juan Pablo López Gross
(Caracas); Ariadne García (Montevideo); Ivonne Patricia León
(Bogotá) and María Belén Fernández Milmanda, Valentina Waisman
and Elliot Sucari (Buenos Aires) have been the best group of assistants that a researcher can have. They prepared the agenda for the
interviews, listened to all the interviews and transcribed them, wrote
some of the reports and literature reviews and managed to work with
two difficult directors who were miles apart.

Many friends and colleagues helped us discover and explore
the fascinating world of politicians. We would like to thank María
Matilde Ollier, John Magdaleno, Carlos de la Torre, Miguel Serna,
Jorge Lanzaro, Alejo Vargas Velásquez, Benigno Alarcón, Osvaldo
Hurtado, Susanne Gratius, Carlos Gervasoni, Enrique Peruzzotti,
Juan Carlos Torre, Lorenza Sebesta, Ernesto Calvo, César Montúfar,
Betty Amores, Normay Wray, Adrián Bonilla, Simón Pachano, Pablo
Celi, Bertha García, Julián González Guyer, Martín Balza, Alberto
Curiel, Arlene Tickner, Francine Jacome, Johanna Mendelson
Formann, Michael Shifter, José Miguel Vivanco, Adam Isacson,
Andrés Serbin, Juan Rial, Domingo Erwin, Heather Booth and Albis
Muñoz.

Mary Ingram helped us with translation and editing. Kika Sroka-
Miller, our editor at Zed Books, has been fabulous, patient and
always happy to help us.

We could not have done our work without the generosity of
our interviewees. We enjoyed every interview. There was a bit of
everything: professionalism, tension, laughter, friendliness and a lot
of information. Some of them opened up their houses to us. Others
waited for us in bars or restaurants. But most of the interviews took
place in government buildings, which allowed us to witness the
beauty of some congresses and houses of government but also to
see much decadence. We want to thank wholeheartedly all of our
interviewees. Both of us have learned a lot from all of them.

INTRODUCTION

> History does not move forward in a straight line but when
> skilled and determined leaders push, it does move forward
>
> Samuel Huntington, *The Third Wave*
> (University of Oklahoma Press, 1992)

Latin America is widely known for its leaders. It is a continent that
has produced political leaders that have gained global recognition –
for good and ill. It is closely associated with leaders whose political
projects have resonated far beyond their own countries. In Argentina,
Juan Domingo Perón inspired a particular kind of nationalist
populism. In Chile, the name of Augusto Pinochet became almost
synonymous with the brutality of military dictatorship. Fidel Castro
still stands as an emblematic figure of revolutionary resistance – and,
for many, of undemocratic rule. In more recent times, Hugo Chávez
developed a leftist project that attracted followers and critics around
the world. The novels of writers like Gabriel García Márquez and
Mario Vargas Llosa have given us memorable literary figures based
on the popular image of the Latin American *caudillo*.

In the last decade, Latin America has experienced a variety of
political trends. And, crucially, the marked differences between Latin
American states have much to do with contrasting leadership styles.
As the region made the transition from dictatorship to democracy
and then into a prolonged debt crisis, the intensity of its challenges
gave birth to very different types of leaders. In Brazil, Uruguay and
Chile, a succession of skilful and consensus-building leaders were

pivotal in laying the foundations for liberal democracy. In Argentina, Ecuador, Bolivia, Nicaragua and Venezuela leaders have taken office on more divisive platforms. In these countries, such leaders command huge numbers of both acolytes and detractors. Love them or hate them, it is undeniable that these men and women[1] have exerted a defining influence over their respective countries' political development.

These twin trends form the subject of this book. First, leadership matters in Latin America, probably more than in any other region. Secondly, a greater diversity of leadership styles has taken root in the region during the last decade. We will show not only how and why leadership styles matter, but that there is a strong link between the structure of party systems and different leadership styles.

A neglected issue

Since the return of democracy to Latin America, there has been an explosion of powerful leaders. However, very little has been written regarding their influence on democratic quality. Surprisingly, despite the fact that Latin America's history is full of strongmen, strong-women and *caudillos*, little attention has been paid to their impact on *how well* democracy works. The list of Latin America's very recent powerful and charismatic leaders includes a military officer, a bishop, a trade unionist, a former *guerrillero* and many women. Their legacies have been complex. Some of them were able to stabilize the economy but to the detriment of political democracy. Some deepened democratic quality but failed in economic management. Others helped to make their societies more equal but undermined civil liberties. Few have been able to achieve economic growth and a more just income distribution without jeopardizing democracy.

This book explores the reasons behind the emergence of different types of leader in post-crisis scenarios. It does this in five Latin American countries. We began the research because we wanted to understand the reasons why the return to democracy has not changed Latin America's tendency to generate extremely dominant leaders. Recently, the region has witnessed the rise and fall of powerful political leaders, alongside the collapse or fragmentation of party systems. Twenty-one presidents were either removed from office or forced to resign from 1985 to 2012. The continent's political class has become the centre of international attention with the emergence of dominant leaders such as Hugo Chávez, Rafael Correa, Álvaro Uribe and Cristina Fernández de Kirchner. Latin America is today associated with certain types of populist leader. Indeed, this is widely seen as the region's distinctive contribution to contemporary political models. While expanding political and social rights, these leaders have polarized political debates and widened divisions between their citizens. This book asks why Latin America has produced such leaders. It finds the explanation in a series of domestic political conditions related to the nature of political parties. We uncover how this lies behind Latin America's modern paradox: the expansion and deterioration of democracy have advanced hand in hand. Indeed, in recent decades, different groups in the region have been included in the democratic game through the expansion of individual rights. This was the case in Bolivia and Ecuador with their indigenous communities and in Venezuela through the inclusion of economically and socially marginalized groups. However, at the same time other pillars of liberal democracy deteriorated, such as the political party system, the separation of powers or freedom of press. Here we understand democracy in its liberal form. It is characterized by fair, free and competitive elections; a political party system, separation of powers and protection of human rights, civil rights and political rights. The pillars of liberal democracy are limited government, horizontal accountability, individual rights and civil liberties. To sum up, a liberal democracy combines open political competition and the protection of individual rights (Held 1996; Youngs 2015).

This is a study of political leadership from different perspectives. First, we review the main concepts of leadership, looking specifically at the relationship between leaders, political context and followers. Secondly, we offer an analysis of political leaders in Latin America which is based on semi-structured interviews with former presidents, former and current vice-presidents, party leaders and legislators. The book draws extensive material from a three-year research project that included field trips, interviews, seminars and publications. The 285 interviews with politicians have provided us with a wealth of information about their ideals, goals, frustrations and perceptions about domestic politics and democracy. The interview material on politicians' perceptions, ideas and beliefs leads into a critical analysis of their performance and democratic quality. Thirdly, the book offers a comparative study of five countries in the region – Argentina, Colombia, Ecuador, Venezuela and Uruguay. Across these case studies, we point to the national conditions that shape different types of leader. In this way, we contribute to a comparative political leadership research agenda which aims to help with theory-building and testing empirical cases (Helms 2012: 9). Fourthly, based on our interviews and primary research, the book provides a new *typology* of democratic leaders.

Situating the debate

Traditionally, academic literature on Latin American studies has focused more on the transition process, the state and economic reforms, the crises of political parties and the phenomena of neoliberalism and populism (Mainwaring and Scully 2010; Fukuyama 2008; Panizza 2005; O'Donnell 1995). Political leadership has been superficially included in the debates about presidentialism and parliamentarism (Diamond et al. 1999). More recently, the concept has gained some prominence owing to the emergence of political representation crises (Linz and Valenzuela 1994; Pérez-Liñán 2009;

Fabbrini 2009). The rise of personalistic and populist leadership styles in Latin America has also been researched (Malamud 2010; Edwards 2009; Philip and Panizza 2011). Conventional wisdom presents this trend as an ideological challenge to liberal democracy led by charismatic individuals.

However, this book suggests that leadership styles in Latin America are better explained if contextualized within the different political party systems of each country. The study analyses the emergence of different types of political leader in Latin America, looking specifically at five countries. These countries were chosen because they have all suffered political and economic crisis – but with very different results. Five presidents were expelled in Argentina, three in Ecuador, one in Venezuela and none in Uruguay and Colombia between 1993 and 2005. Analysts argue that 'crisis offer excellent opportunities for studying political leadership in action' (Boin et al. 2012: 119). Crises are unique moments at which 'who leads matter' (Lord 2003: xiii). This book argues that some countries of the region, in post-crisis scenarios, seem to have fallen into a political trap marked by strong leaders who are democratically elected but once in power devote themselves to corrupting the political regime and maintaining themselves in power.

Locating itself within debates over the quality of democracy, this book looks at the relationship between leadership styles and broader political processes. Good-quality democracy is like an extremely intricate and finely tuned machine. When working to perfection, the machine produces high-quality output. But much effort is needed to build the machine and get it working properly, and its very complexity leaves it vulnerable to breakdown. The temptation is to look for a shortcut. Voters turn to leaders who promise solutions without going through the tortuous process of building such an elaborate and fragile machine. Their very impatience to see democracy's promises fulfilled installs leaders with an impoverished understanding of democracy's machinery. This study is concerned with the operators of democracy, those responsible for the quality of the product. It is about those who are in charge of what we might call 'democracy craft'. We start from the assumption that the importance of leaders in the working of democracy is paramount and that they should be considered as pivotal for understanding the widespread deterioration in democratic quality. They should also be recognized when they enhance democracy.

In addition to the above, this book also examines the challenges encountered by the authors in conducting research in five different countries; fixing interviews with politicians and listening to them. The book offers both a critical analysis of political leaders and the vicissitudes of interpreting a politician's words. Thus, based on interviews with politicians, this book narrates what politicians who are currently in office think about democracy, their role, their impact and ideas. When politicians are currently under so much scrutiny and criticism, this book explains the conditions that allow so many 'bad' politicians to survive in domestic politics and able to diminish democracy. The book combines analyses with a narrative on the challenges posed by such research in political science.

What will follow

The main contributions of this book are a typology of democratic leaders; a qualitative analysis of 285 interviews with political leaders; and the story behind the management of a research project.

The book has six chapters. Chapter 1 describes the making of the research project. In 2008 we began to discuss the predicaments of political leaders in Latin America. It took us around one year to put together a research project. In this chapter we narrate the different steps of this process: How did we formulate different research questions and hypotheses? Why did we choose to interview politicians? How did we organize the questionnaires?

In 2009 the project was approved by the Foundation of Open Society Institute in Washington, DC. Thanks to this grant we were able to conduct 285 interviews in five capital cities with former presidents, former vice-presidents, incumbent vice-presidents, legislators and party leaders. The interviews were conducted between 2009 and 2012.

The first chapter has two main aims. It explains our research method and presents the problems that a researcher encounters when analysing political leaders. The chapter does not offer a pure academic perspective. Rather it tells the story behind a four-year project which was managed by one director in Buenos Aires, another director in Madrid and a team of seven research assistants in different countries. Our purpose is to discuss the main difficulties found during the development of the project. Thus the chapter offers ideas about the design of the interviews, the dichotomy between qualitative and quantitative approaches and the management of a huge flow of information coming from literature reviews, interviews and seminars.

Chapter 2 outlines our conceptualization of political leadership. Following mainstream debates on political leadership, we discuss definitions of leaders, context and followers. The chapter explores the Latin American context and offers brief analysis of the political scenarios of the five case studies. Based on a qualitative analysis of the 285 interviews conducted in Caracas, Bogotá, Buenos Aires, Montevideo and Quito, the chapter offers a typology of democratic leaders. The typology was articulated by putting together different institutional settings and the characteristics of leaders which were discussed in the interviews.

Chapters 3, 4 and 5 test the typology in Uruguay and Colombia, Argentina and Ecuador, and Venezuela, respectively. We decided to divide the case studies according to their institutional settings. Therefore, Uruguay and Colombia are analysed together since their political party system has a high degree of institutionalization. Argentina and Ecuador are studied in Chapter 4 as two cases in which the degree of institutionalization of the party system is low. Venezuela is examined in Chapter 5. There are three main reasons why Venezuela is a case on its own. First, we were not able to interview Chávez's followers. We contacted members of the Partido Socialista Unido de Venezuela (PSUV), legislators from the party, journalists and academics who had a pro-Chávez stand but none of them accepted to be interviewed. Therefore the interviews were biased. Moreover, we arrived in Caracas when news about President Hugo Chávez's health were released. The interviews were monopolized by current affairs. It was a big effort to try to follow our questionnaire. Secondly, Venezuela was the only country from our basket which underwent a collapse of its political party system. Lastly, Hugo Chávez as a political leader was unique.

These three chapters are very different. In the case of Uruguay and Colombia, the interviews were not monopolized by discussions about one particular leader. In Uruguay, our interviewees gave us interesting quotes that we reproduce anonymously. But they were reluctant to provide a detailed analysis of José Mujica's leadership. They perceived political leadership as a collective phenomenon. In the case of Colombia, there were many references to the different styles of leadership of Álvaro Uribe and Juan Manuel Santos. However, most of our respondents emphasize the analysis of the political context in which leadership is exercised. Indeed, the issue of political violence monopolized the interviews.

In the case of Argentina and Ecuador, the interviews were more concentrated on the analysis of the leadership of Néstor Kirchner, Cristina Fernández de Kirchner and Rafael Correa. Issues such as clientelism, populism and strong presidentialism were discussed in almost all interviews. Thus, the responses of our interviewees allow us to offer some quantitative analysis. During the interviews, some policies were discussed as examples of how leadership was exercised. We have included some analysis of these policies, which has also helped us to structure our typology of leaders.

The chapter on Venezuela is a combination of a study of policies, especially those that were discussed in the interviews, and a qualitative analysis of the interviews. As we said, the interviews in Caracas were monopolized by the leadership of Hugo Chávez, his illness and the February 2012 primary elections. We made an effort to discuss how leadership could be exercised by the younger politicians who have created the new political parties.

Therefore, there are differences in how each case study is presented. Rather than trying to standardize the analysis, we prefer to respect the differences that emerge from the interviews. We believe that these differences enrich the comparative analysis.

Chapter 6 discusses the conclusions of our research and further explores the value of our typology. The evidence presented here has uncovered a complex and fluid relationship which indicates that the degree of political party institutionalization and the forms of political competition influence leadership styles. The key element is the degree of autonomy that leaders can carve out in contexts of over- or low institutionalization of political parties. Listening to politicians in Argentina and Ecuador, it became clear that leaders have a notable capacity to ignore rules and citizens' demands by building clientelist networks and concentrating power in their own hands. In Uruguay, politicians are held accountable by their parties and their autonomy is limited. In Venezuela, Hugo Chávez has been able to rewrite the institutions of the state, concentrate power in his hands and hollow out state power. In Colombia, the political system is contaminated by violence. The institutions of the state and the degree of institutionalization of the political party system are still able to control political leaders. Paradoxically, they can avoid concentration of power but they cannot avoid corruption and violence.

The book argues that certain political conditions allow for the emergence of different types of leader. It offers a new typology of democratic leaders that highlights their impact on the quality of democracy.

CHAPTER 1

How to Study Leaders

Introduction

Our research was motivated by questions about the democratic quality of political leaders in Latin America. How could leaders who had successfully established democracy in their countries take political paths that would lead to a gradual deterioration of the quality of the democratic institutions? What motivates some leaders to employ populist, clientelistic methods to build or strengthen their power? Why are so many young politicians so naive and inefficient that they quickly lose power?

We observed different type of leaders in Latin America. We wanted to discover why in some countries excellent democratic leaders emerge while in others populist, inefficient or corrupt leaders prevail. The literature suggests a combination of elements linked to the historical and cultural context, the strength of state institutions and the extent of democratic practice among the citizens of the country in question. What we did not find were texts that laid out the thinking of politicians themselves. Therefore we decided to interview politicians. We wanted to know their perspective on the democratic quality of political leaders and the political conditions that help the emergence of different types of leader.

We knew, then, what we wanted to do but still had to decide how to carry out the research. Therefore we consulted both books and experts. Before we coordinated the interviews we undertook a literature review. Our first discovery was that there is very little written about leadership in academic texts, especially in Latin American political science. Although one of the classic texts on leadership, *The Prince* by Niccolò Machiavelli, had recognized the importance of leaders in any political project, modern political science had concentrated more on the structure of parliaments, political party systems, elections and the relations between the branches of state power, omitting the subject of leadership.

We also discovered that most of the literature on leadership was in the field of business studies, concentrating on private sector performance. Although some of the ideas in these studies can be applied to our field, we needed a different approach. In studies on business, negotiation and strategy, there are a lot of resources on both the study and training of leaders. But this material cannot really be applied to the study of political leaders. There are major differences between leading businesses and leading countries. Typically studies on leadership focus on an analysis of the personalities of the individuals. However, they tend to be more of a psychological examination of their good and bad points rather than a political discussion. Our interest was shared by other academics who had started to investigate the subject of leadership more systematically (Lord 2003; Kellerman 2004, 2012; Bueno de Mesquita and Smith 2011; Nye 2008; Helms 2012).

In order to establish a line of questioning for future interviews we carried out a series of informal meetings with colleagues in Buenos Aires and Madrid, and ran the questions by opinion poll specialists for their input. Thinking about questions for future interviewees was the first concrete task of this research. The project was taking shape. We wrote it up and submitted it to different foundations. In August

2009 the Foundation Open Society Institute in Washington, DC, approved our project and in October we started work.

The study took four years and covered five different cases, which enabled us to offer comparative analysis. It entailed ten study trips, 319 interviews in six countries, seven seminars organized in Toronto, Buenos Aires, Quito and Madrid, the writing of research reports, work documents and journalistic articles, the editing of a book in Spanish, and finally the writing of this book.[1] It involved a team of seven research assistants in five countries.

Here we intend to discuss how we organized our material and conducted the research. This chapter is not strictly methodological. It is not always easy to implement what methodological texts stipulate. Often the researcher changes their hypothesis, variables and ideas and in many cases this means starting again from scratch. We had to grapple with social science methodological rules, but what we seek to convey stems more from concrete experience than scientific theories.

This chapter also covers the unexpected elements that any social scientist can encounter when they seek to explain political reality.

Defining our hypothesis and case studies

The initial hypothesis of this research holds that the deep-rooted authoritarian tradition in Latin America protected those in power from having to engage in any real deep and meaningful transformation of the democratic system. A consequence of this, we maintain, was the destruction of any new democratic leadership. Our assumption was that the traditional modes of behaviour such as clientelism, *caudillismo*, authoritarianism, the desire to hold on to power indefinitely, and corruption helped to explain the numerous political crises which have been the scourge of the region throughout the last three decades. Other countries, by contrast, worked to institutionalize political systems that broadened democracy.

Given that this is a rather sweeping assumption, we set out from the beginning to compare different cases in order to be able to reach some generalization, since, as Morlino says, 'comparison makes it possible to control for the hypothesis' (Morlino 1991: 14). In addition, a comparative study helps to construct assumptions and identify trends that we hoped would shed some light on how change could improve the democratic quality of leaders.

The examples we chose adhered to traditional comparative criteria, i.e. cases with similarities as well as differences. We used the Mill difference method (Pérez-Liñán 2007: 8–10) to identify cases in which we assumed that the leadership was democratic and others in which we held that the leadership characteristics were less democratic.

To begin with, we took a series of social phenomena which we considered to be tied to the rise of different types of leadership, as were the crises, the problems of political representation and the fragmentation of political parties. Our dependent variable was initially the democratic quality of the political leaders. As a first step in the research we defined democratic quality by taking as a basis the study by Barreda, which measures this quality as a function of five dimensions: 1) political rights and civil liberties; 2) responsiveness of the government; 3) level of participation; 4) accountability; and 5) rule of law, or rather the validity of the legal system (Barreda 2011: 270).

However, as our research progressed, we modified our initial hypothesis and refocused the study. We argue that the quality of the democracy could be considered as a product of the type of leadership and thus we began to focus more on the different types of leader. What we observed was that many Latin American leaders were elected democratically but once in power they seek to destroy the institutions and democratic processes, establishing legal frameworks to enable them to remain in power. Many of them succeeded, others came up against the power of the institutions themselves or popular discontent. This diversity suggests that the political context could explain the emergence of different types of democratic leaders. One of the factors that seems to have explanatory power was the degree of institutionalization of the political party system.

With these early observations and an extensive bibliographical review we began to formulate a different hypothesis: i.e. the quality of the leaders could be related to the degree of institutionalization of the political parties and of the state. This hypothesis enabled us to focus on the variance of the leaders. Leaders do not rise from a vacuum, so we assumed that the different institutional arrangements promoted the emergence of different types of leaders (the independent variable). In addition, since a leader has to win over supporters so as to become a leader, the second independent variable was the relationship that the leader established with the voters. Hence we began our study of political leaders with the assumption that leadership has three components: the leader, the followers and the context, as per Figure 1.1.

The next step was to define each category. In order to explore different elements of the leadership relationship we took five dimensions: a) how leaders entered politics; b) whether they had a suitable

FIGURE 1.1 Hypothesis

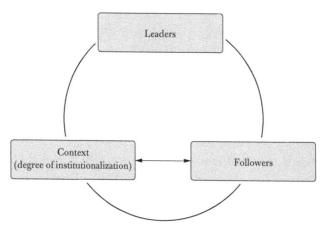

FIGURE 1.2 Dimensions of leadership

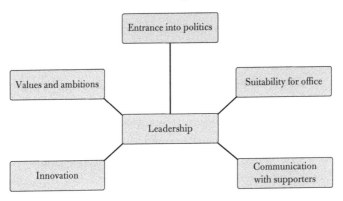

background for holding an executive or legislative position; c) their values and ambitions; d) the relationship with their followers and the media; and e) their readiness to innovate and use new technology (Figure 1.2).

With regard to context, we reviewed the literature on the subject of the institutionalization of political systems, a topic which has been widely covered. In particular, following Mainwaring and Scully (1995), Alcántara (2004) and Ollier (2008, 2013), we used the concepts of high and low institutionalization of political parties. First, a party system is institutionalized when parties have continuity in terms of internal rules and inter-party competition procedures. Secondly, institutionalized parties are well established in society and have ideological consistency. They generate ideas, programmes, proposals and government plans that allow citizens to understand the party's aims. Thirdly, parties are the vehicle for political representation, providing a legitimate way to gain access to government. They are also a vehicle for representing interests; they are channels for interest groups to make their voices heard. Fourthly, the internal organization of institutionalized parties is coherent with efficient instruments for internal discipline to avoid and punish corruption

(Mainwaring and Scully 1995; Alcántara 2004). Analysts have concluded that institutionalization does not guarantee high-quality democratic institutions, but that a low degree of institutionalization weakens any type of democracy (Mainwaring and Scully 1995: 21). A non-institutionalized party system increases the chances of arbitrary decisions being taken. If the parties are weak, or the rules are not clear and transparent, force, violence or mass movements become ways to gain power and access to government. If rules and procedures are flexible and change constantly, the system leaves room for manipulation, which in turn benefits parties or leaders, thus ruining the political and legal pillars of a democratic system. Parties can be hijacked by interest groups, which end up gaining privileged access to government posts or influence over the decision-making process. This amplifies the differences between interest groups and citizens, and makes the system unjust rather than democratic. A low degree of institutionalization also increases the likelihood of a personalist, populist leader coming to power, particularly in presidential systems (Mainwaring and Scully 1995: 22). If the system is obscure and party discipline is erratic, the level of autonomy can easily increase. Here we understand politicians' autonomy as their capacity to be isolated from citizens, political parties and/or to 'make decisions at odds with citizen demands' (Fukuyama 2013: 10).

Measurement of followers/supporters was more complicated since we did not want to limit ourselves solely to the relationship between populist leaders and their supporters. In order that we could consider different levels of adherence to leaders, we used concepts tested in interviews. They referred to three aspects which stem from the concept of participation (Hagopian 2005: 41–90): the type of communication (personal, media, only in political campaigns, group, individual); aim of the link (electoral, permanent, intermittent); and the transparency of the management. We also tested the way in which advisers are incorporated as another source of link with supporters (see Figure 1.3).

FIGURE 1.3 The leader–supporter relationship

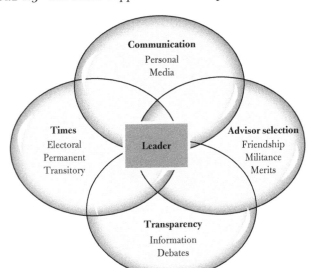

The second stage was to choose the case studies (Deslauriers 2004: 31). We began by selecting Argentina and Ecuador. Both countries had undergone major political chaos with presidential crisis, exhaustion of the party system and questioning on the part of society. Secondly, we chose Uruguay and Colombia, because they share some characteristics, such as having undergone crisis situations and changes in their two-party systems while maintaining a stable party system and consistent, lasting political careers. Lastly, we chose Venezuela, which was quite unique, with a major political crisis followed by the emergence of a strong leader who was able to secure political stability (see Table 1.1). We would have liked to have included more cases for comparison since broader studies in the field of social sciences enable the formulation of generalized classifications. However, our project had a set amount of financing which forced us to balance academic criteria with

TABLE 1.1 Selection criteria for the case studies

	Variables				
Cases	Party changes	Stable party system	Rules for the rise of leaders	Criticisms from society	Turnover of presidents
Argentina	YES	NO	YES	YES	YES
Ecuador	YES	NO	NO	YES	YES
Colombia	YES	YES	YES	YES	NO
Uruguay	YES	YES	YES	NO	NO
Venezuela	YES	NO	NO	YES	NO

concrete reality. We had to discard research on Brazil, Chile and Peru, all of which was very interesting. There was only a limited time to carry out the research and this did not stretch to more than the five cases we chose. As Patton stated, 'having weighed the evidence and considered the alternatives, evaluators and primary stakeholders make their sampling decisions, sometimes painfully, but always with the recognition that there are no perfect designs' (Patton 1990: 181).

All the cases have one common characteristic and lack one of the other attributes (Pérez-Liñán 2007: 9–13). Following qualitatively oriented comparative methods, our aim was to compare the conditions or causes in different historical contexts with a holistic and interpretative approach. Our ultimate purpose was to understand and interpret the differences and similarities in political leadership issues in the region. We believe that by focusing our comparison on the similarities and differences between our case studies, they 'can tell us a great deal about the way governments function' (Peters 1998).

The design of the research and of the sample

The research project posed many methodological questions. From the start we opted to conduct a comparative, qualitative study. We argue that a qualitative study is more relevant for social science (Flick 2012: 15). However, we accept that, gradually, studies in political science have become more embedded in different methods of quantitative research. Despite the dominance of quantitative studies, social scientists tend to consider it more useful to use a qualitative approach when dealing with a limited number of cases (Morlino 1991: 16–17). Moreover, the originality of this research lies in the information produced by the interviews with politicians. We wanted to use the narrative of the interviews, the stories that were told and the impressions that were given rather than limit ourselves to a quantitative approach.

However, the qualitative analysis exhibited some problems as well as benefits. Given especially the nature of the comparative case study, we tried to control 'the sources of variance in the ex-ante selection of the cases, rather than through ex-post manipulation of data' (Peters 1998). In other words, we endeavoured to make the sample as representative as possible, by analysing the political representation of parliaments in each case study. However, we confronted some significant issues about the conceptualization of the sample.

One of the main challenges was to define who would fall into the category of political leader. The choice led to many controversies in the early discussions. One classification which involved a very small margin of error was legislators. They constitute a relatively homogeneous universe and therefore an averagely rigorous sample. In addition it was a reasonably fair sample since their numbers are in proportion to support for their political party.

However, as is often the case in social science, reconciling methodology with reality is not easy. First, there are important differences among the legislators. There are some who have been elected many times and others who are in their first term in Congress. Some are close to the press and their ideas are better known by the general public. Others can be good political operators within their parties but have limited visibility. Being a national deputy who represents a large district with a large electorate is not the same as being a national deputy representing a province with few inhabitants. Some legislators have held important positions in the executive or high-ranking party positions, while others are new to the political game. In fact, a distribution of the interviewees by party membership, reflecting the percentage obtained in elections, does not necessarily ensure a fair distribution in their universe as a function of the objectives we had established.

Secondly, as indicated by Taylor and Bogdan (1987: 36), it was not possible to determine beforehand who would fit into that universe. This means that for each of the five cases we could draw up a table that illustrates representation criteria as a function of the votes obtained by each political party. We could consider those criteria with information from the media to compare legislators with a greater public exposure with those who are either new or less well known. We could also include the degree of involvement in executive power. But we could not guarantee that the legislators we chose were actually prepared to be interviewed, and many of them were not. Although we had identified our universe, many of those selected did not answer our requests for interview. We were therefore concerned that we would end up with an arbitrary sample which would make it difficult to extrapolate results and establish causal relationships (Gerring 2008: 156–7).

One way of dealing with this problem was to select a universe that was not based on a proportional sample but that considered well-known people in the political sphere. This was the solution we chose, and we consider that despite the problems with regard to distribution, it was easier to achieve a balanced representation. Given that we could not obtain a balanced representation of political parties according to their distribution in Congress, we opted to choose leaders as a function of their importance in terms of the political agenda. Hence we decided to increase our sample to include political leaders both in parliament and outside it. This involved another benefit because we realized that we could not confine our concept of political leader to the purely legislative and we wanted the opportunity to interview politicians in the executive and party apparatus.

The definition of this universe was closely related to the method involved in deciding on the population of our study. Our approach was to speak with ten colleagues in each of the five countries with whom we had worked previously. We asked them to provide a list of the ten most politically influential people and leaders who had had a distinguished political career. We also asked them to provide us with contact details for the individuals, such as their telephone numbers, email addresses and name of the institution they belonged to. We appreciated that the data could be skewed by virtue of the relationship with our contact, where they worked or the political party they belonged to. Hence we spent time comparing the list with the local press to be sure that the political leaders our contacts had suggested did indeed appear frequently in the local news. We also applied a specific time frame and regional spread so that we were not simply including politicians in the capital cities of the countries involved. We also included local academic specialists in the field of political science and political journalists who could help us draw an accurate picture of the political scene pertaining at the time of the interviews.

We were aware of the bias that could creep into our sample given our use of such heterogeneous criteria. However, in line with Azorín and Crespo (1986: 69), we believe that the 'the optimal design of the sample could only be achieved by relying on knowledge of the population'. As is widely accepted in the social sciences, similarities between the components of the universe are not previously given properties but distinctions made by the

observer (Mandujano Bustamante 1998: 3; Salgado 1990: 349).
Therefore, having defined in basic terms the characteristics of
those we wanted to make up our universe, we chose cases that met
those conditions according to the information provided by opinion
pollsters, key contributors and local leaders. This was an intentional
sample (Patton 1990: 100–105; Deslauriers 2004: 58; Pla 1999: 296),
derived from a theoretical concept.

The lists could easily contain over 200 names. Hence we decided
to organize a ranking according to the number of times the person
had been suggested by our colleagues, and this cut the list down to
sixty individuals.

Then our assistants began the difficult job of trying to find a way
of speaking with the potential interviewees by internet or telephone.
The research assistants compiled information from public sources
to build up a complete profile of each candidate. This helped to
guard against any bias towards specific political parties.

We told all the people that we contacted that we had been given
their name by an important source. Since it is difficult to gain
access to politicians we realized that more influential sources could
open more doors for us as well as foster a greater degree of trust
between ourselves and the interviewee (Taylor and Bogdan 1987: 38;
Deslauriers 2004: 39–40). This worked well in most countries apart
from Venezuela. We did not experience many difficulties in speaking to the politicians on the lists. Unless they had no space in their
diaries or were travelling, the politicians were happy to speak to us,
again with the exception of Venezuela.

We asked the people who responded positively and quickly to
us whether they could also suggest names of people we could interview. This also meant we avoided omitting relevant people so we
had a greater understanding of the domestic political process in
each country (Gerring 2008: 181–3).

While in the letters to our colleagues we explained our objectives
and asked for their help in designing the interviews, in the letters to

interviewees we included a summary of our project and the aim of the interviews, emphasizing that our work was purely for academic purposes and that we would not publish anything without their prior approval. Recording the interviews tended to create a degree of tension. We tried to mitigate against this by stating firmly that they would not be quoted, nor would any other personal characteristics be mentioned that would identify them. As Flick has noted, recording people's speech reveals things about them that it is difficult to control (Flick 2012: 68), and following Taylor and Bogdan's recommendations (1987: 80–81) we also took written notes if the person made a specifically pertinent comment.

The method of choosing the universe cannot be optimal in terms of its methodological validity (Elster 2010: 218–19; Deslauriers 2004: 28–30). However, we made an a priori classification of the categories to define the interviewees and we respected those criteria in the interviews. In each country we planned between forty and forty-five interviews with legislators, party leaders and politicians who had been or who were in the executive. We also interviewed between ten and fifteen academics and journalists who helped us to identify and interpret political trends, social problems, issues on the domestic agenda, etc. These were very important in helping us to illustrate the institutional background against which the leaders were operating. Most of the interviews were carried out during our study trips. Others were carried out by our local assistants. This brought the average number of interviews up to ninety per country.[2]

Interviews were largely carried out in a single week. Our local assistants accompanied us to the interviews, which helped to systematize the type of interview we wanted and to train them so that they could do the job themselves. Since we had so little time in each place, the agenda was packed. We undertook between seven and eight interviews a day, some together and some separately. At the end of each day we evaluated our observations. We read notes and discussed any doubts so that we could make any necessary changes for the next day's interviews. Then, as recommended by López Estrada and Deslauriers (2011: 12): 'it is very important to write up the notes immediately after each interview. For that to be possible, the transcript should be considered part of the interview itself. The passage of time, contacts with other people and doing other activities can act against us. We should remember that we forget quickly.'

Many of the leaders we contacted wanted more information about the reason for the interviews. Some wanted to have the questions in advance, but we tried not to comply with this as it would detract from our aim of having an open discussion in which the interviewees could freely express themselves. We had taken into consideration Jon Elster's suggestion. He said that 'explaining behaviour is often in the situation and not in the person' (Elster 2010: 206). In other words, answers formulated in advance by the interviewee (or their adviser) put a distance between the two people when the actual interview takes place. It is also worth mentioning the variety of places where the interviews took place: an office in Congress, a personal office, party headquarters or, as happened in Caracas, our hotel to avoid being punished for speaking to foreigners.

Carrying out the interviews

An important aim of our work was to instil a degree of confidence in us on the part of the interviewees so that they would be prepared to answer our questions frankly. As they had not met us beforehand, we ran the risk, as is usual in interviews, that we would give off the wrong signal about what our real objectives were. There was not very much that we could really do to gain their trust other than being punctual, thanking them for meeting us, showing an interest in listening to them and avoiding any sort of prejudice or criticizing what they said (López Estrada and Deslauriers 2011: 9–12). Some of the meetings were long and rather heated. Others constituted the bare minimum to comply with having offered to do the interview at all. Altogether we can attest that they were very enriching.

We learned something from every interview. Most politicians want to be known and are expansive by nature. They were concerned about reaching out to their supporters and establishing good communications. This was helpful, and most of the interviews ended up being very long conversations about their political careers, their values and how they saw the prevailing climate. A major issue for them is how to stay in power or at the very least how to stay in politics. They do not want to disappear. Hence the media constitutes a valuable resource for them to spread their political message. Some had mistaken us for journalists and were disappointed that we were not. Appearing in the media was of more interest to them than being in an academic report.

We also came to appreciate their limitations. In some cases we were surprised at the lack of knowledge that many had about international affairs and their rather parochial outlook. In a lot of cases there was a marked inability to criticize themselves.

In light of our results, we are happy with the way we conducted the interviews. As López Estrada and Deslauriers (2011: 1, 6–7) point out, 'the interview has enormous potential to allow us to reach the mentality of people, but also to gain access to their vital side so we learn about their daily life and social relationships'. We were extremely careful about choosing topics of conversation that would allow us to collect a lot of data so that we could evaluate and analyse their political careers. Our aim was to listen to the politicians; hence the interviews were semi-structured around open-ended questions, so as to give interviewees the opportunity to speak extensively about their careers and domestic politics. In each case we started with a question that allowed the interviewee to speak without too many interruptions. However, although we did not stick rigidly to the questionnaires, we did want to repeat a few formal well-defined questions in order to encourage each speaker to talk about topics that interested them.

If we had not had some similarities in the questioning, we would not have discovered the indicators that enabled us to establish comparisons and generalize about the leaders of the region.

The process of putting together the interview had a number of aspects. Since there was no agreement in the literature about the qualities of a political leader, the selection criteria came from our own conceptualization of the topic more than from secondary sources that dealt with similar subjects.

The categories of questions

We chose five themes to help us identify what sort of leader we were interviewing. They were: a) their entry into politics; b) their qualification to hold an executive or legislative position; c) their values and ambitions; d) their relationship with their supporters and the media; and e) their ability to innovate and use technology. We could explain in detail how we chose the five categories but it seems more important to point out that while we used a set format for the interviews, we did change the questions somewhat, adding some which came from previous conversations and leaving aside topics that did not generate interesting material.

The data were difficult to group together: 'a problem may be that narrative material is generally not linear, and paragraphs from transcribed interviews may contain elements relating to several categories' (Elo and Kyngäs 2008: 113). Bearing in mind that 'codification is a means of deconstructing data: the researcher takes an element of information, removes it and isolates it, classifies it with others of the same type, deindividualises it, decontextualises it' (Deslauriers 2004: 70), the five themes we present largely comply with the evaluations that came up in the interviews. Thus codification reproduces the data according to codes derived from the material collected during the project or rather built on the responses of the interviewees and the framework of our survey.

With regard to how they entered politics, and in line with Kane and Patapan (2012: 4), we were interested to know whether their nomination as a candidate stemmed from political competition, since that is an essential characteristic of a democratic regime. It was also important to us to ascertain how important the interviewee considered that question to be. In other words we wanted to know whether the interviewee made any reference to the legitimacy with which they held their position.

In examining access to politics, we wanted to know whether they had had a mentor, whether they came from a political family, how they had won their first public office and what qualities they thought they had to have been selected. On this point there were considerable similarities between older politicians. It was quite common for them to have started their political career in university militancy, and their replies referred to role models that had influenced their development as well as things they had read. Meanwhile, the younger interviewees tended to belong to social organizations and not to have role models or any particularly inspiring texts.

In the chart below (Figure 1.4) we can see that university militancy was a frequent channel into political life. Except for Uruguay, which has rather fixed rules governing a career in a political party, in the other three cases (Argentina, Colombia and Ecuador) it is the main source of entry into politics. In Venezuela it did not have a marked influence. This can possibly be attributed to the fact that traditionally entry into politics was via the two traditional political parties (COPEI and Acción Democrática). In addition the sample from this country includes hardly any official legislators, so the issue of access for new leaders does not represent the new generations of politicians who emerged during the presidencies of Hugo Chávez.

We were also interested in what training or preparation they had had to carry out an executive or legislative job. Our questions referred to the necessary qualities for the job as well as characteristics they considered most important for their career. Was education

FIGURE 1.4   Access to their first political post

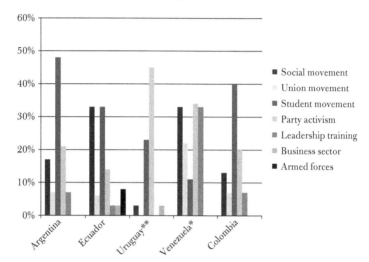

*   In Venezuela we were able to interview only politicians from the opposition parties. Therefore this chart does not include those who come from the armed forces.
** In Uruguay a high percentage (26 per cent) come into politics because of family relations.
N = 285

or practical experience more important? Did it require them to have done a similar type of job or was political militancy more valuable? It is worth emphasizing that we did not start out with an elitist idea of leadership qualities, we did not have any prejudices with regard to university education, and we valued equally a politician from a union organization or local militancy. In the few cases where the legislators or politicians had started their careers in trade unions, there was a generational difference. The older ones stressed the effect of reading and political debate while the younger ones talked only of militancy.

We also asked whether they had had any formal training to prepare them for a political career, since one assumption of our research was that schools of leadership do not really influence political careers.

The third item in the interviews, analysis of values and ambitions, aims to analyse what aspects of their political activity they value most and what topics involved in the game of democratic politics are important to the interviewee. For example, we asked how they built consensus between party members and with the opposition, knowing that if we asked whether it was important to seek consensus we would obviously get a positive answer. Going against the expectations of the interviewee was always risky (Taylor and Bogdan 1987: 72–4). Politicians know what is correct. However, we found on various occasions that politicians were so sincere they harmed themselves. For instance, some politicians told us without any shame that they had engaged in some financial shenanigans to gain their position, that they had gained it thanks to nepotism or that they had no single quality to justify holding their current position.

At this stage we introduced questions about how they valued democracy. We tried to get the leaders to talk about democracy. We were interested to see what the politicians understood by democracy, what ideas they had about everyday democracy and how they experienced democracy in their daily life. We understood that 'the vision for democracy is a fundamental characteristic of democratic leadership since it creates the environment that leaders and followers pursue to improve their society and nation in terms of the demand for democracy' (Choi 2007: 251).

Table 1.2 shows the degree of understanding of democracy among the leaders. A high percentage (between 39 and 51 per cent) considers democracy a guarantor of power division. In Venezuela, as a consequence of the social rhetoric of the twenty-first century, most emphasized the importance of protecting minorities. The lowest percentage relates to responses about guaranteeing political management. This was not really considered an important characteristic of democracy by many of the leaders. The answers were more diverse than these five categories, but despite the variations it was possible to group them.

TABLE 1.2 How the leaders assess democracy

	Guarantees division of power	Guarantees political representation	Guarantees political management	Guarantees protection for minorities
Argentina	49%	25%	19%	7%
Ecuador	48%	26%	26%	n.a
Uruguay	51%	33%	4%	12%
Venezuela	50%	n.a	n.a	50%
Colombia	39%	21%	20%	20%

$N = 285$

On the subject of valuing democracy, we introduced questions about populism and clientelism as ways of exercising leadership. We expected the leaders to respond that these political practices were negative, in line with the tacit consensus that predominates in Western democracies. In order to avoid any false responses, the questions covered issues such as what elements would be lost in the relationship with activists and voters if we put to one side clientelistic policies. Who would be most affected if we limited excessively clientelistic practices? How would you respond to the concrete demands of supporters?

Finally we also asked about the role of political parties and whether that had changed or whether they kept the same party traditions. What effect had the political party had on their political career? How did they feel the political party had contributed positively or negatively to their career? We asked how they defined their electorate and the mechanisms the party employed to support their candidates. We also explored ideas about the formation of alternative policies and how politicians who changed party were considered.

With regard to their supporters and the media, in order to discover how the respondents understood the making of politics, we included questions about their everyday routine, communication with their constituents and the process of selection of their advisers. We asked whether they met with their supporters personally, how many they saw a month and how they managed follow-up to their requests. In order to assess their openness to new forms of making politics, we asked questions about generational change, gender and class.

Most studies on leadership have neglected to consider the importance of supporters in empowering or limiting leaders. For us, supporters play a fundamental role, especially in countries where the institutions are weak, the political parties are in disarray and leaders tend to concentrate power in their own hands. The recent presidential crises in the region have shown that 'informed citizens no longer accept the role of passive audience. They want to be actors, not spectators' (Darcy de Oliveira 2008: 120). Therefore the interviews gave the politicians the opportunity to talk about their experiences with their supporters and to expand upon the relations they had with them at a personal level and via social networks. Other questions referred to how they chose to communicate with voters.

With regard to how they put together a team, we started by asking how many assistants they had, what functions they performed and how they had contacted them. In just two instances out of 285 people we interviewed did they choose their assistants via open competition. This point was very telling. As for their advisers, the legislators did not seem to believe in any sort of democratic, open and transparent method to choose them. Legislators select their advisers from among their political party, their friends or relatives. In a few exceptional cases the respondents mentioned taking into account technical or intellectual ability. After the interviews, we reached the conclusion that how they put together their team of advisers is a good indicator of how democratic the leader is.

Finally the interviews also included questions about innovation and use of technology. We wanted to know whether the respondent was aware of changes in political debates, and whether they felt that society was demanding a different discourse. Most of the politicians used new technology, web pages, Twitter and Facebook, but the majority could not really say how they benefited from them or how they could gain the most from these tools.[3] Although this technology creates dynamic interaction and we tend to believe that it democratizes politics, the leaders we interviewed continued to hold that the more traditional ways of recruiting party members and supporters were the best. Many indicated that nothing could replace face-to-face contact and walking through neighbourhoods to reach out to potential supporters despite technological progress. Many said that they left it to their younger advisers to communicate with voters and make use of technology.

The interviews were long. Few lasted less than an hour. Some of the leaders talked at great length about their careers, others talked more about democratic and political values, and others were almost incapable of sticking to the questionnaire, preferring instead to talk about current domestic political issues. It is not our intention here to narrate the 285 interviews at length. Nevertheless, the following pages encapsulate the most interesting findings, presenting our respondents' ideas about their political career and the qualities of political leaders.

Politicians' perceptions

The first question in the interviews was 'Why did you enter politics?' This question gave politicians the chance to talk about their political career. In many cases, especially in Argentina, Colombia and Uruguay, the opportunity to get into politics is related to family connections. Our respondents emphasized that they were born into a Peronist family, a Liberal family or a Colorado family. Very few of them rebelled and followed the opposition. One Colombian senator from the Conservative Party said that he started out in politics when he was twelve years old. Many of them discovered their ability to lead a group from an early age in school. The word 'vocation' came up in the majority of the interviews. In the five countries the majority of our respondents explained that they understood politics as social service. Legislators from rural areas mostly entered politics through community service in their towns. Particularly in Colombia, many respondents stressed that they entered politics to help their country to end political violence. In Venezuela, the younger politicians entered politics to oppose Hugo Chávez.

We were aware of the fact that our respondents could reply with answers they believed created a good impression. Probably this is why many replies were 'I entered politics because I had a vocation for public service', 'I wanted to end injustice' or 'I wanted to improve the life in my community'. Many respondents argued that their personal aims were of secondary importance and that their main objective was to serve the community. Yet the majority of our respondents did seem to believe that they had a real vocation for public service.

The second question was 'How and why did you get your first job in politics?' Sixty-three per cent of the respondents in Argentina said that it was militancy either in university or in their political party which opened the door for their first job. Thirty-four per cent said that their first job came through personal relations. In Ecuador, 65 per cent pointed out that they got their first job through militancy in the parties, university or a social movement. Forty-five per cent of our Uruguayan respondents told us that it was through militancy in political parties and 23 per cent through activism in university. In Venezuela 34 per cent got their first job thanks to militancy in political parties, 33 per cent in social movements and 11 per cent in university. In Colombia 40 per cent of our interviewees got their first job through militancy in political parties and 36 per cent thanks to family connections.

Talking about personal qualities necessary to become leaders, the respondents gave very different answers. We have grouped them in two categories: personal qualities and militancy. In the first group, the following answers appeared repeatedly in the majority of the interviews: intuition, strong personality, hard worker, willpower, good oratory skills and persuasiveness. In Uruguay honesty was mentioned many times as a quality and a need. In the case of Argentina, politicians were very critical, highlighting the problems rather than the qualities. One legislator said that politicians were very arrogant and that the Congress was a 'bonfire of vanities'. In the second group of answers, the most common replies referred to ideological coherence, many years of militancy in the party and the ability to create consensus and to talk to political opponents. Other answers that were interesting included: 'my brother is the governor', 'my father's death opened the door to attain the national level' or 'female quotas opened the door'.

Charisma was also widely discussed in the interviews. Most of our respondents did not consider charisma as something extraordinary. It seems for them that most leaders in the region have some degree of charisma. They associated charisma with high popularity and a strong personality. The dark side of charisma was also brought up in the interviews. Many respondents argued that many of their colleagues become arrogant, individualist and selfish.

Another quality which was mentioned in the interviews was the capacity to debate. A senator in Uruguay said that political debate helps to define personal positions, to clarify ideological preferences and to manifest your values.

A young *Asambleísta* in Ecuador recognized the lack of political training and formation among the new generation of leaders by pointing out that 'we need to discuss concepts, ideologies and political traditions, we need to build a government plan, to study the current situation and to plan the short-term future'. We found that the absence of training and formation was a feature of all the countries considered in this study. Despite the fact that there are a significant number of schools organized by political parties, social movements, international organizations and churches, our respondents agreed that young militants and politicians do not have proper training and formation. This was a more acute concern in Argentina and Ecuador because of the recent renovations that opened the door to younger generations of politicians. Respondents in Colombia and Uruguay recognized that a political career was more structured and thus politicians were gaining experience over time.

We also asked about communication with followers. Most of our respondents said that they were active on Facebook and Twitter. According to our research, the majority of our interviewees used the platform to upload activities and promote themselves but they were not very interactive with the followers. It was very common to hear expressions about preferring the old type of communications and the face-to-face meetings. We were told by many respondents in our five countries that 'the main political theatre is the street'; 'to be in the street with the people is our aim'; 'in politics you have to be connected to people'; 'political parties have to be closer to the people'. The younger generation was more inclined to combine the internet platforms and the personal contact with followers.

Having discussed leaders' qualities, we asked about leaders' deficiencies. The shortfalls mentioned most often were in relation to honesty, ethics, tolerance and transparency. Some of the respondents suggested that to improve the democratic quality of leaders it was necessary to tackle corruption and increase accountability and transparency in private affairs. Thirty-six per cent thought that the separation between the public and private spheres should be clearer.

One of the last questions which actually sprang more out of curiosity than methodology was to ask whether any other family member (partner, children, brothers or sisters) was in politics. This produced some surprising answers. Some said that they would not consider it a good choice for their children to go into the same profession.

From that we deduced that they considered a career in politics to be rather negative and that they did not want their children to experience problems similar to theirs. In other cases it was surprising how many family members had had political careers, demonstrating both nepotism and power dynasties. In only a few cases did a respondent express regret that nobody had followed in their footsteps.

In one of the most important questions we gave our respondents the opportunity to explain how they conceptualized democracy. In every country more than 30 per cent replied that democracy is a regime that guarantees division of power. One member of PAIS in Ecuador said that 'democracy can ensure that the executive does not interfere with the legislative'. Democracy was also considered a guarantor of political representation and protection of minorities.

Unanimously democracy was named as the best form of government. In Ecuador, 69 per cent of the respondents argued that democracy can control leaders. One *Asambleísta* said 'democracy need citizens who are well informed'. In Colombia the emphasis was on democracy as a political regime with tolerance and transparency. It was also pointed out that democracy should promote a clear division between private and public affairs. In Uruguay, 40 per cent of respondents argued that democracy guarantees political representation and 20 per cent that it protects all political ideologies. In Argentina, politicians talked about accountability and consensus. Finally, in Venezuela, democracy was seen as a political regime that promotes tolerance.

Legislators in their buildings

Politicians know that when they speak they should show some vocation to work for the public good. In an interview, the leader knows what they should say to be perceived positively by an interviewer. However, we found other ways to assess political leaders. For the most part the interviews with legislators took place in parliamentary buildings. We visited legislative palaces and annexes, since both contained parliamentary offices. Some legislators had their own private offices whilst others met us at their party headquarters. We learned a lot about democracy in each of the countries simply by seeing these buildings and observing the way people worked.

The most modern parliamentary building is in Ecuador. The National Assembly in Ecuador is a new building which replaced the Congress that burnt down in March 2003. It is a modern, light, transparent building with large windows. Its modernity contrasts starkly with the run-down area in which it is situated. The legislators' offices are bright and spacious. The Assembly was a very dynamic space with corridors full of legislators, advisers and journalists and offices full of visitors and people in meetings. It was easy to get into the building despite the usual identity checks. Some of the offices had open spaces where commissions could hold meetings. In some instances, while we were waiting to speak to people, we felt as though we were participating in the meetings as they were held with the doors open. All of this gave us the feeling that this building was an accessible space. We were well received in the Asamblea Nacional, the members gave us their time and hospitality without any problem. Beyond customary Andean friendliness, the Ecuadorean interviewees exemplified the existing polarization in the country and were very clear as to whether they were in favour or against the government of Rafael Correa.

The Argentine Congress has two main buildings: the Palace and the Annexe. The Palace is an imposing building with a green dome. It is opposite but some distance away from the Casa Rosada, which is the headquarters of the executive. The Annexe is in front of the Palace and is a modern, tall, largely glass building. We went to both the Palace and the Annexe and both gave us a similar impression. One afternoon in September 2010 we were waiting in the part of the Palace where the senators have their offices. It is an old grand building with very high ceilings and a magnificent wide marble staircase.

We were asked to sit in a huge room just outside the senator's office. The leather chairs were old, broken and dirty but we sat down anyway. While we waited we looked at the lights on the staircase and one of us asked quietly, 'Who stole the lampshade?' Another one of us looked at the oak door and asked, 'And who stole the door handle?' On that floor, in the waiting room, there were neither lampshades nor door handles. We had not lost our past glory but had probably stolen it from ourselves. Who are the people who take things from the Senate? They must be Argentines because we found it hard to believe that a foreigner would come into this building to take a few mementos. Do they put the things on display in their homes like trophies? Do their family and friends look proudly at the lampshades and door handles stolen from the Senate? Is nobody ashamed of this stupid robbery?

If the Palace had a sort of faded glory from another time that we will never recover, the Annexe embodies more current misery. The air-conditioning pipes are bare and dirty. The lifts suggest that they are not maintained regularly. On leaving the lift on any of the floors you are faced with a labyrinth of corridors that have few signs and are dark, dirty, hostile and unkempt. The offices of the deputies are small with narrow staircases and are rather claustrophobic. The degree of deterioration and dirt in the legislative offices surprised us and showed us the neglect that has been introduced into Argentine politics during the years of democracy. One senator told us how difficult it was even to get the curtains in his office washed. Nobody seemed to care about the dirt, the dust or what had happened to the lampshades. Argentina, like its legislative buildings, is going through a bad time politically and old contradictions are mixing with constant neglect. Stealing a lampshade or enriching oneself illegally to the tune of a million dollars goes unnoticed. We had the feeling that in Argentine politics nobody cared about anything.

In Uruguay there is also a Palace and an Annexe. The Palace is quite similar to the one in Argentina and has a sunny internal patio with arabesques and paintings. The building is well looked after and clean. The Annexe is a rectangular building with five floors. When you reach any of the floors there is a person to show you where the legislator's office is. Off the hall there are wide welcoming corridors with comfortable clean seats that do not have holes in them. All the offices which lead on to this corridor have windows, so it is possible to see all the people who work with the legislators. These wide corridors act like impromptu meeting rooms, where you see different legislators talking, having mate, making coffee. They walk past each other and greet each other there, including us when we were waiting to be seen. We met with the legislators we had interviewed in these corridors and they greeted us pleasantly. The Annexe is a simple, clean, welcoming building. These wide corridors encourage people to greet each other and to talk. They are places where everyone knows everyone else; they understand and respect each other. The building is like Uruguayan politics because, as the legislators repeated over and over again to us, they all know each other and that helps to keep corruption under control; nobody wants to stand out and they like to talk until they come to an agreement. The Annexe and the Palace in Montevideo show a Uruguayan political culture that is friendly, respectful and which encourages dialogue. In the corridors there was a feeling of camaraderie and respect. There were no missing lamp-shades or door handles and the buildings are surrounded by wide avenues, as in the rest of the city. The respect and harmony in both buildings reflect the style of doing politics in Uruguay.

The parliamentary office in Colombia also has an imposing structure, like a traditional court. Wide corridors link the legislators' offices and everything is well looked after. As in the Ecuadorean Assembly there is an atmosphere of intense activity and dynamism with the obvious sense of camaraderie that was so palpable in the Uruguayan parliament. The interviews with left-wing legislators included in some cases heartbreaking anecdotes about threats, exile or assassinations. There was a grief and sadness among some left-wing representatives that was impossible to ignore. Many of the interviews were rather like confessions. The harsh political struggle in Colombia heavily influenced our conversations with legislators. This also had an impact on the security measures required to enter the parliamentary offices. These controls and mistrust permeate the Colombian political game.

Venezuela was a very special case. The governing party officials would not speak to us, nor would any of the opposition legislators speak to us in the Congress. Most of the interviews took place in our hotel. Some opposition legislators admitted that they did not want to be seen with foreign interviewers. We had to spend time convincing a lot of the opposition legislators that our work was academic rather than journalistic. One of the people we interviewed stated that because we were backed by a US organization official party politicians would not speak to us. Consequently we did not visit the Congress or the offices of any legislators. The cessation of the political game and social fragmentation stopped us from evaluating this political space.

If the buildings reveal aspects of the prevailing democracy in each of the countries we visited, we have no hesitation in stating that the best-functioning democracy was in Uruguay. Second place would go to Colombia, with the proviso that many of the stories we heard inside the buildings showed that democracy is a façade for a terribly unequal, unjust and violent regime. Ecuador showed a contradictory face – a new transparent building in a deteriorating neighbourhood. This contrast enabled us to see the paradox of contemporary Ecuador, where the new mixes with the old, where the renewal promised by Rafael Correa involves many of the old guard. It has become another *caudillista*, clientelistic government within which it is only possible to see a few new elements. It was the Argentine Congress which had the worst effect on us. It appeared to be frozen in time between past glory and present misery. Venezuela left us rather frustrated as we could not get to know anybody with any parliamentary power – if that indeed exists there. Their buildings were closed to us.

At the beginning we had never thought that buildings would contribute to our study. We had not anticipated that in our initial debates, nor was it included in our questionnaires. It was, however, a helpful factor that supported our other findings. The buildings said a great deal about the political game in each country. This was obvious. Often theories do not take into account such observations, as Deslauriers (2004: 86) pointed out: 'above all qualitative research seeks to show that grand theories can be shown as useless if they are prisoners of a conceptual framework'. Nonetheless, an open-minded, attentive researcher can find useful data in facts and situations that do not correspond to more traditional classifications and which have a tremendous richness.

Conclusions

This chapter explains how we carried out the research. It is not a traditional methodological chapter. Our aim is to show the real process of preparing and carrying out research about political leaders.

We began by addressing the main motivation that has driven this research: the democratic quality of political leaders in Latin America. We explained the different hypotheses that we developed and how the literature review helped us to refocus the study. One of the most important findings of this stage of the research was the need to contextualize the study of leaders historically.

The chapter also described the process of selecting the case studies. We wanted to explore political leadership in stable and unstable political contexts, and therefore we chose five case studies which provided us with a variety of scenarios.

The design of the research, methodological questions and doubts about the sample were also discussed with the aim of explaining the difficulties that we encountered.

We also offered an analysis of the interviews and of the way in which we articulated the questions. We have included some analysis about why the interviewees enter politics, their personal ambitions and aspirations, and their relationship with their followers.

The interviews were the pillar of our research. The opportunities to meet with former presidents, former vice-presidents and legislators gave us a unique opportunity to analyse political leaders. We also discovered that the parliament buildings provide some ideas about the political context. From a personal standpoint, we had the chance to meet 285 leaders, many of whom had been very important actors in the politics of their respective countries. We learned a great deal about them, and many of them engendered in us a rather sad disappointment. Altogether, though, it was a very enriching experience which we have outlined in these pages.

With all this material we faced a huge challenge: how to unravel ideas about leaders and democratic quality from almost 600 hours of conversation? This was a tough task, and we present the main contours in the following pages. We discovered that our respondents connected leaders to legal frameworks, opposition and power. Thus we have articulated different models of democratic leaders taking into account these three elements. In the following pages, the reader will find a suggested classification of democratic leaders.

CHAPTER 2

Models of Democratic Leadership

Introduction

The premise of this book is that the quality of leaders is fundamental to the overall performance of political regimes. We understand leadership as a power relationship between an individual and a group of followers established in a concrete historical context. Leaders can transform the context, and persuade followers to accept change. Leaders in democratic countries can enhance or undermine democracy. In this chapter we offer a new typology of democratic leaders which takes into account the impact that leaders can have on the quality of democracy.

The chapter is divided into four sections. The first section discusses definitions of leaders and analyses their relation with followers and the context in which they operate. The second section presents the context of our research. Based on the interviews, this section briefly analyses the political scenarios in which leadership is exercised in Argentina, Colombia, Ecuador, Venezuela and Uruguay. It also studies the main political trends that can help us to explain the reasons for the emergence of new powerful leaders. The third section studies different typologies of leaders and presents a new typology based on the conclusions of our research. It offers a typology of leaders based on different institutional settings. Indeed, we depart from the assumption that 'context plays a relevant and unavoidable role in democratic leadership' (Teles 2013: 13). The last section concludes with a discussion of the relationship between the context and the emergence of different types of leader.

The leader, the followers and the context

A leader is a person who leads a group of people, a country or an organization. The leader defines the agenda and motivates the group to follow it. In general terms, leaders give directions and provide solutions to common problems. There are many definitions of leadership but most of them include more or less the same pillars: power, influence, inspiration, guidance, vision, ability to understand the context, to diagnose weaknesses and strengths and to set the agenda with goals and effective solutions.

Political leadership is the ability to influence, motivate and inspire. An individual becomes a political leader because he is able to modify the course of events (Blondel 1987). A leader should be able to make a difference, and to influence his followers' attitudes, beliefs, demands and needs (Masciulli et al. 2009). He has to have the capacity to interpret citizens' aspirations and to understand the national interest. He needs to motivate citizens to follow him. He must be capable of understanding the historical context, the complexity of different political scenarios and the alternative solutions available. The leader has to interpret the problems, prescribe ends and means to solve them. The leader has to present his personal visions to attract and mobilize followers (ibid.). A leader should be able to 'bend' the context and his followers (Teles 2013: 5). However, his power has to be limited by the institutions of the state and the followers. Powerless institutions and/or followers make political leadership unpredictable and probably undemocratic.

As suggested by Nye (2008), the leader has to create the group, set the agenda and the strategy to achieve it. He has to help to build the group's identity. However, a leader can also emerge from a group of people who have coalesced around specific objectives. In this case, the leader has to accept the challenge and set the strategy to achieve the goals.

Analysts have also agreed that the definition of political leadership has strong cultural and historical contextual components. These components should be taken into account when political leadership is defined and analysed (Masciulli et al. 2009). It has also been argued that political leadership should be studied historically and comparatively (Teles 2013: 1).

The leadership literature endows a democratic leader with a significant number of qualities. A democratic leader is identified as an individual who has vision, courage to innovate, integrity, intelligence, shrewd judgement, tolerance, flexibility, the ability to implement changes and absorb information, to interpret different views and to build consensus (ibid.; Brown 2014).

There is no leader without power or followers because a leader exists if and only if there is a group of people that supports his agenda. Leadership and power go together, establishing an asymmetrical relationship: 'political leadership implies holding a certain "amount of power", but the opposite is not true – it is possible to have power (for instance, in hierarchical relations) without being a leader' (Teles 2012: 117). Power has been defined many times before. Lukes' (2005) definition understands power as the capacity to make or resist changes. Dahl (1961) explains power as the ability to make others do what they would not have done otherwise. This could be achieved by coercion or persuasion. These different approaches divide power, according to Nye (2008), into hard and soft power. The first is identified with threats or privileges and it is used to make others change their actions, attitudes and or/decisions. On the other hand, soft power is the capacity to obtain results by inducement and persuasion with no manipulation. Soft power seems to be an essential attribute of a democratic leader. Nye (ibid.) argues that effective leadership requires a combination of soft and hard power, known as smart power.

As there is no leader without followers, even bad leaders have them. The followers have a crucial role in monitoring what the leader does, pushing for transformation or abandoning the leader. People follow leaders for different reasons. In politics, we follow leaders in the hope that they can solve our problems and manage public goods. They give us a political identity and ideals. They are inspirational and persuade us that they know how to govern. Bittner (2011) argues that followers evaluate leaders according to two main factors: character (looking at honesty and compassion) and competence (looking at intelligence and strength). There are important biases in the way followers perceive political leaders. In general terms, leaders from conservative parties seem to be considered more competent while left-wing leaders are seen to have more honesty and compassion (ibid.).

Thus, followers matter; their role is crucial in legitimizing, passively or actively, both good and bad leaders. In order to understand the emergence and endurance of bad leaders, followers are as relevant as the leaders themselves. Above all, followers matter because 'those who can bring a leader to power can also bring the leader down' (Bueno de Mesquita and Smith 2011: 59). Hirschman (1970) conceptualizes followers' attitudes as exit, voice and loyalty. Through these, followers seem to have the key to discarding a bad leader. The main problem is that, in the literature, leaders remain overvalued and followers undervalued, despite the fact that followers are crucial to limiting leaders' powers, especially now with the spread of information (Kellerman 2012). If followers abandon the leader, then he loses power and the leadership relationship is gone. The followers are no longer there to legitimize the leader's authority.

Leadership studies tend to concentrate on the 'strongman', paradoxically proclaiming what they want to avoid, which is the cult of the leader (Burns 1978). This is closely related to the personalization of politics. Teles (2013: 3) points to a set of changes that have helped the process of personalization: institutions accord more relevance to individual politicians than to collectivities; electoral campaigns are centred on individuals; politics is understood as a competition between leaders and political preferences are formed by individual political actors. This trend had already been highlighted by Fabbrini (2009) when he confronted the increasing power of the democratic Prince with the deterioration of political parties. Both studies attempt to emphasize that the political leader makes a difference. This is the case in strongly controlled democracies where the systems of checks and balances work, but much more so in countries with weak institutions. We argue that, in an institutionally weak political scenario, some political leaders can become necessary causes, understood as the 'outcome would not have occurred if the cause had been absent' (Mahoney et al. 2009: 118). Following Barrington Moore's idea of 'no bourgeoisie, no democracy', can it be argued 'no Chávez, no *Revolución Bolivariana*' or 'no Correa, no *Revolución Ciudadana*?' We advance the idea that there is a combination of political factors that help the emergence of a political leader and help him to become a necessary cause. Taking into consideration the five countries that we study for this book, we would suggest that the degree of institutionalization of political parties seems to be a crucial factor with explanatory power.

If the leader is an individual who has power and is in charge of creating a group, an identity, an agenda and a strategy, what or who creates a leader? For some analysts a leader is an individual born with specific abilities that can be developed in school, the workplace or in a political environment. Others would argue that a leader emerges thanks to historical conjunctures (Tucker 1977). The classical example given for the latter is Winston Churchill, who was a secondary politician in Great Britain until the beginning of Second World War. Our analysis should be placed within the latter category since we aim to observe the different domestic political factors that promote the emergence of different types of leaders in Latin America. In this book we are interested in exploring the political conjunctures that inspire the emergence of different leaders. As Masciulli et al. (2009) argue, leadership is a historically concrete phenomenon. Therefore, the research needs to take into consideration beliefs, values, characters, power relations, ethical and unethical values, attitudes and actions of formal and informal institutions. Thus, the historical and cultural-institutional context is essential to analyse patterns of political leadership (Nye 2008). As Kellerman (2004: xiv) puts it, 'leadership does not take place in a vacuum. All leader–follower stories are set in the particular contexts within which they unfold.' We followed two debates that help us to highlight the need for the contextualization of leaders. The halo effect (Thorndike 1920a, 1920b) explains that a leader can be praised or demonized to such an extent that is impossible to assess his achievements or failures in a balanced way. Thus, our perception of a leader can be contaminated by making inferences on the basis of a general impression (Rosenzweig 2007). Indeed, we could judge the leader by the country's economic performance, simply accepting the idea that achieving economic growth is the outcome of a good leadership and an economic recession the outcome of a bad one. The halo effect can be very damaging because it can compromise our analysis. The romance of leadership (Meindl et al. 1985) can also undermine the objectivity of the study. This was particularly important as we were analysing political leaders in a region which historically has a messianic view of leadership. Because of the interviews, we faced the risk of understanding events only in terms of leadership. In other words we risked being biased in associating leaders only with political outcomes in a positive or negative sense. We argue that the contextualization of leadership helps us to overcome this risk. Most importantly, we selected our interviewees from different political backgrounds which contributed to our receiving different perceptions of leaders and political processes. Despite our precautions, the study of leaders is always risky and can easily be influenced by the halo effect or a romantic perspective. There is a higher risk when political leadership is studied in regions with long traditions of strong leaders. The halo effect was omnipresent in the interviews in Venezuela and Ecuador, where society has been deeply polarized by Hugo Chávez and Rafael Correa, respectively. To place the leaders in their political context improves the chances of avoiding a romantic perspective.

Through 285 interviews with political leaders in Latin America, we aim to understand and explain the historical and cultural-institutional context in which leadership is exercised and to explore the political causes that explain the emergence of different types of leaders. We observe that in Latin America, the political context is mainly dominated by historically powerful leaders, mobilized followers and weak institutions.

The scenario of our research

Since 1985, and owing to social revolts or parliamentary pressure, twenty-one Latin American presidents have left government abruptly.[1] In this context, the democratic deficit or the gap between citizens' aspirations and their level of satisfaction increases. In many countries, democracy may be seen as the preferred form of government, but in many states society remains 'deeply sceptical when evaluating how democracy works' (Norris 2011: 5). In Latin America 79 per cent of citizens believe that democracy is the best political regime but only 57 per cent of them are satisfied with its results (Latinobarómetro 2013). While followers may have been able to provoke the fall of presidents, they have not managed to avoid the re-emergence of deep-rooted political practices under subsequent administrations. Thus, presidential crises in Latin America showed that followers can get rid of bad presidents but have been unable to ensure that the newcomer will be any better. Therefore one of our questions is why followers could be wise enough to dismiss bad leaders but not sagacious enough to prevent the access of new bad leaders.

The context of our research is marked by the post-presidential crises scenario in Latin America. In our region presidents stand out. Presidential leaders matter more in presidential and semi-presidential regimes and even more under majoritarian electoral systems and two-party systems (Webb et al. 2012). It has been argued that presidents have become 'guardians of the laws and symbols of national values' (Lord 2003: xii). Citizens look to presidents for justice and inspiration and, therefore, the character of presidents, their values, beliefs, behaviour, traditions and ideas, matters. When all these seem to have become extremely relevant, the 'personal integrity in our leaders seems both more fragile and more necessary than ever' (ibid.: xii).

The recent presidential crises seemed to be a short-term solution but did not solve the long-term democratic deficit. We have identified a significant fault in most Latin American democracies: there are no clear paths for the formation of democratic leaders and no tools to avoid undemocratic, dishonest and/or inefficient leaders being elected. Political parties have been losing ground as the institutions which enable politicians to gain expertise and be selected for public office. As Fabbrini (2009) has pointed out, there has been a process whereby power has increased for individual politicians but deteriorated for political parties. This process, previously known as presidentialization, had already been identified by Juan Linz (1990). His analysis highlighted presidentialism's rigidity. Linz (ibid.: 55) argued that in time of crisis the negative risks of presidentialism increase, 'ranging from the death of the incumbent to serious errors in judgment committed under the pressure of unruly circumstances'. Thus presidential rule is less predictable and often weaker than alternatives. Increasing presidential powers makes the president stronger and the risks higher. Presidentialism, combined with extraordinary powers, places the destiny of the nation in the hands of one individual and Linz (ibid.: 69) cleverly pointed out that 'heavy reliance on the personal qualities of a political leader ... is a risky course'. Latin America provides too many examples of presidentialism under different conceptualizations, such as *caudillismo* or populism. Indeed, in Latin America extreme presidentialism has gone hand in hand with populism and a low degree of institutionalization. The recent presidential crisis deepened this situation. The fall of presidents affected the political parties more than the leaders themselves. In fact, in many cases the legacy of the presidential crisis was the emergence of another strong leader.

In Latin America our context is dominated by historically powerful leaders, mobilized followers and weak institutional settings. This was the scenario presented to us in the interviews. With the exception of our Uruguayan respondents, the interviewees refer to powerful presidents when asked about leaders. Presidents concentrate executive power and in many cases they usurp power from other institutions, especially the legislative. Presidents in Latin America disempower the institutions to empower themselves. The followers deify or hate them, and politics is played in the extremes of a very polarized society in which democracy becomes blurred.

Our research led us to conclude that some Latin American countries seem to have fallen into a political trap: weakly institutionalized regimes undermine political competition which in turn helps leaders increase their autonomy and subsequently the quality of democracy deteriorates. Leaders become autonomous and democracy becomes dependent on their actions. This trap was described in many of the 285 interviews undertaken for this study: the logic behind it seems to be that concentration of power, despite its negative consequences, secures political stability.

For the purpose of this study, Argentina, Colombia, Ecuador, Venezuela and Uruguay were chosen because all suffered similar deep political and/or economic crises. However, the outcomes were different: five presidents were expelled in Argentina, three in Ecuador, one in Venezuela and none in Uruguay and Colombia. In Argentina, Ecuador and Venezuela the crises brought about the fragmentation or collapse of the party systems and the emergence of strong leaders. Economic crises became political crises. In contrast, in Uruguay the 2002 crisis neither affected the political party system nor did it become a political crisis. However, the traditional political parties lost the elections and the Frente Amplio won the presidency for the first time since its creation in 1971, without affecting the political system. Colombia's long conflict has been managed with a high degree of institutionalization of its political party system and an inexplicable level of political stability. While the political parties underwent important transformation following the constitutional reform of 1991 and the 2003 political reform, political stability and a high degree of institutionalization allowed a strong leader such as Álvaro Uribe to come to power but also helped to control his political ambitions.

In Latin America the majority of political parties have not modernized following the transition to democracy. Of course, the parties have assumed the defence of democracy as one of their main pillars but most of them have been unable to democratize their internal institutions and internal organization, their ways of accessing power, debates and discourse. Many parties lack advisory teams or think tanks that could structure their political thought, strategies, tactics and an agenda for government. Some of the political parties are mere electoral machines, organized around one strong leader. If we believe that democracy still functions through political parties, their problems will be seen to cause a low-quality democracy and will be reflected in the poverty of public policies and agendas for government. The deterioration of political parties makes a low-quality democracy more likely.

The decay of political parties is concealed by the emergence (or the construction) of charismatic leaders (OEA and PNUD 2009). Many Latin American political parties, rather than control or monitor their leaders, deify them and provide them with a wealth of power resources. Leaders are increasing their power while political parties are fading away (Fabbrini 2009). In electoral campaigns, leaders seemed to have replaced parties and debates. Indeed, elections are more related to the personal characteristics of leaders than to the policies and government objectives that they represent. Most of the messages seem to be ambiguous, made for a television audience rather than for politically aware citizens. In this context, populist leaders spread. While political parties are unable or unwilling to control or monitor their leaders, populism and clientelism seem to expand and flourish.

State institutions are also crucial in overseeing democratic leaders' behaviour. If institutions legitimize leadership, they should be able to monitor it. The formal institutions of the state have been considered, mainly by John Locke, as tools to secure the rights of the led (Kellerman 2004: 16). The institutions should have the capacity to restrain the power of the leader. The combination of powerful leaders and weak institutions distorts the pillars of liberal democracy. The institutions' weakness increases expectations of leaders' capacity to solve the problems that the political system has been unable to clear up. Citizens look for powerful leaders to compensate for the weakness of the formal institutions of a political regime. But in the long term, strong leaders become an obstacle to the strengthening of formal institutions. Indeed, strong political leaders may well not find incentives to empower institutions that could control or monitor their activities. In Latin America, most of the strong leaders have not worked towards the strengthening of formal political institutions.

By the end of the 1990s, politics in Latin America altered with the emergence of new, populist, leaders. Here we analyse only some conceptualizations of populism since leadership can adopt many populist forms. There are too many definitions of populism and, paradoxically, some analysts argue that it is a difficult political phenomenon to grasp. Germani's (1965, 1971) definition is still very influential. Populism was conceptualized as a stage on the path towards modernization that basically helped to include the working class in politics. De la Torre (2008) offers three historical categories: classical populism, which was born out of the import substitution industrialization process; neopopulism, which was the product of the end of industrialization and the implementation of neoliberal policies; and radical populism, which emerged with the collapse of neoliberalism. The former president of Brazil, Fernando Henrique Cardoso, argues that populism means the exercise of power without institutional mediation or control. It is mainly based on the direct relationship between the leader and the followers, which is based on the exchange of political or social goods (Botana 2006). Other analysts have interpreted populism as a tendency to reduce the number of veto players in politics and the power of institutional control (Navia and Walker 2010).

In order to understand populism, analysts have traditionally related this political phenomenon to economic inequality. Most of the works presented by De la Torre and Peruzzotti (2008) argue that populism emerges when an economically dominant elite perpetuates itself in power. Therefore, populism is understood as a response to that political and economic domination.

Here we argue that the leader is crucial in the development of a populist model. Without a leader, populism cannot flourish. Usually the populist leader has some degree of charisma. The discourse of a populist leader builds a strong polarization between 'them and us'. While populism is presented as a political tool for inclusion and a vehicle for change, in recent decades populism has been unable to generate long-lasting wealth redistribution. Despite its revolutionary rhetoric, populism has not produced deep transformations in economic structures. However, it has persisted since it established a political regime that allows millions of citizens to have access to social goods. The Venezuelan case is the best example of this.

This phenomenon goes hand in hand with clientelism. Citizens receive social benefits in exchange for political loyalty (Abente Brun and Diamond 2014). Leaders receive votes in exchange for the distribution of social or other benefits. The equation means that both actors win and thus there are no incentives for change.

Our research reveals powerful leaders who most of the time use populism and clientelism to increase and maintain power. These powerful leaders usually usurp power from other institutions of the state, manipulate the rules and weaken democracy. Followers are polarized – while some support the leader, others hate him. Their political participation can be either controlled by the leader or non-existent. However, when crises hit, followers are ready to expel the leader, looking for another saviour. Their participation in political parties had declined but they fill the streets to support their new leader or to show their discontent.

The makers of democracy in Latin America seem to be more worried about their role in the political process than in the end result of the process. Rather than working to improve the quality of democracy, the majority of political leaders seem to be more concerned with increasing their share of power to achieve a privileged position. Leaders in Latin America think of power as hard power, democracy as concentration of power in the executive and leadership as requiring a strong political figure who can surpass the limits imposed by laws and institutions. According to one of our respondents politics has become a 'bonfire of vanities' and leaders seem to be more important than democracy.

Categorizing the leaders

Inevitably, when studying leaders, the researcher is inundated by ethical ideas about good and bad, right and wrong. Nye's contribution (2008) is related to the conceptualization of the word good: a leader can be good in moral terms or according to his degree of efficiency.

Even if the goals are morally wrong, the leader could still be considered good if he is able to achieve them. He could be efficient but morally wrong. On the contrary, good leadership should be good both ethically and instrumentally. Unfortunately we have to agree with Masciulli et al. (2009) that 'if we decide to limit the studied universe of leaders by weeding out all tyrants, egoistic "power-wielders" and morally deficient individuals, the remaining number of cases might be too few from which to draw any meaningful conclusions'.

The number of typologies of leaders has recently increased, especially those that differentiate leaders in the private sector (Harvard Business School 2011; Kellerman 2004; Nye 2008). Typologies help us to categorize objects or subjects. In the case of leaders, they help us to put some logical order among the different types that have traits in common or that are extremely different. To put some order into the varieties of leaders helps us to discover trends and foresee the influence that leaders could have at the national or international level. Typologies help us to draw a map of differences and similarities in the emergence and the performance of leaders.

A classical typology of leaders was designed by Aristotle drawing a line between self-interested leaders and common-interested leaders (Table 2.1). His typology is based on the number of leaders, their motivation and result. His typology is a valued-based, nominal typology.

TABLE 2.1 Self-interested and common-interested leaders

Number of leaders	Motivation and result	
	Self-interested	Common-interested
One	Tyranny	Kingship
Few	Oligarchy	Aristocracy
Many	Democracy	Polity

SOURCE: Masciulli et al. (2009)

The difference between attempting to reach self-interest and common interest can correlate to what Kellerman (2004: 34) calls ethical and unethical leadership. The ethical leader put his followers' needs before his own, has private virtues such as courage and temperance and exercises his leadership in the interests of the common good. Bueno de Mesquita and Smith (2011: xviii) present a more brutal argument by which 'politics is about getting and keeping political power. It is not about the general welfare of "We, the people".' By analysing dictators and exploring the reason why 'bad behavior is almost always good politics', they argue that politics is about individuals, each motivated to do what is good for them, not what is good for others (ibid.: xix). Therefore, from their perspective, there is no leader who is willing to achieve only the common interest unless it implies also achieving self-interest.

Other typologies of leader, outlined by Max Weber (1984), Burns (1978) and Deutsch (1990), are more related to the functioning of the leadership relation. Max Weber organized his typology around his idea of the different types of domination. Thus, there are different types of leaders according to the kind of domination that they exert: traditional, rational-legal or charismatic. The most studied one is the charismatic domination, in which the leader is gifted with extraordinary powers and is able to transform the political scenario. James MacGregor Burns (1978) identifies two basic types: the transactional and the transforming. Most of the leadership relations are transactional: leaders and followers exchange one thing for another such as jobs for votes, or tax benefits for campaign contributions. The transforming leader aims to satisfy higher needs and engages the follower fully. The result is a relationship of mutual stimulation. Deutsch's typology is simpler since it divides the leaders according to the power resources they hold: strong and weak (Deutsch 1990). Kellerman (2004) offers a typology of bad leaders that includes seven different types: incompetent, rigid, intemperate, callous, corrupt, insular and evil. However, she also argues that there are two

main categories: 'bad as ineffective and bad as unethical' (ibid.: 32).
Most ineffective leaders are judged such because of the means they
employ to follow their goals. In general, most leaders define reason-
able objectives but fail to reach them.

We offer a new typology of democratic leaders which has been
built through a qualitative analysis of the 285 interviews conducted
in Bogotá, Buenos Aires, Caracas, Montevideo and Quito. In order
to build up the typology, we have analysed three elements: the political context, the ability of the leader to lead and the impact of the
leader on the quality of democracy. We developed a typology which
is based on three dimensions: the relationship between the leader
and the rule of law; his efforts to achieve consensus or to provoke
polarization and his methods of increasing power. Our typology of
democratic leaders is normative with an emphasis on the impact that
leaders can have on democratic quality.

From the analysis of the interviews, we have identified four different groups of democratic leaders: democracy enhancers, ambivalent
democrats, soft power usurpers and power usurpers.

Democracy enhancers include leaders who push for the building or reinforcement of democratic institutions, accept power limits
imposed by state institutions, respect and promote democratic rights
and civil liberties and leave their posts on time. They are usually
inclined to share power and responsibility, build consensus and
avoid polarization. This type of leader belongs to a political party
in which he has developed his career. The party tends to maintain
its principles and norms and has some internal rules to monitor the
performance of its members. Therefore, democracy enhancers are
not autonomous. Following Aristotle's typology, these are leaders
who aim to enhance the common interest. According to Kellerman's idea, they are ethical leaders. Democracy enhancers are more
inclined to use soft power. They are categorized as rule develop-
ers, bridge builders and respectful of the limits imposed by state
institutions (Table 2.2).

TABLE 2.2   The democracy enhancer

Rule developer	Pushes for the building or reinforcement of democratic institutions
	Promotes and respects horizontal accountability
	Promotes and respects democratic rights and civil liberties
	Respects freedom of the press
Bridge builder	Builds consensus
	Tolerant
	Works with his cabinet
	Inclined to share power and responsibility
Respectful	Accepts power limits imposed by state institutions
	Leaves his post on time

The ambivalent democrat respects people's rights, works in a cooperative manner but seeks to accumulate personal power. This type of leader believes that strengthening his position requires negotiation and making concessions. He is able to work in a team and can work with the opposition. However, the ambivalent democrat has a clear tendency to accumulate power. The leader accepts normative regulations but gives himself a leading role in their application. Unlike the democracy enhancer he respects but does not strengthen democratic institutions. The ambivalent democrat can actually end up weakening democracy in his bid to increase his own personal power. He follows rules and is a receptive leader and a soft challenger (Table 2.3).

The soft power usurper navigates between challenging and accepting the rule of law and state institutions. The historical context becomes crucial since it can allow or block the leader's ability to gain autonomy. In crises, the collapse of party systems, situations of extreme violence or abrupt changes in the international context, this politician can take advantage of these exceptional phenomena to reduce the scope for action of other institutions. However, at some

TABLE 2.3   The ambivalent democrat

Rule-obedient	Respects democratic rights and civil liberties
	Respects freedom of the press
	Respects horizontal accountability
Receptive	Accepts consensus
	Relatively tolerant
	Works with his cabinet
	Sporadically works with the opposition
Soft challenger	Challenges power limits imposed by state institutions
	Agrees to share power and responsibility
	Leaves his post on time

point in this power-building process, a break is applied by his party, the judiciary, the legislative power or even societal pressure. On these occasions the soft power usurper retreats in the hope of new favourable conditions arising that will enable him to fit the political game to his own personal or collective aims. Nevertheless, this retreat is never total, so each new advance is a step towards a greater degree of autonomy than at the beginning. The leader is conscious of his strategy and knows that at some stage he will be able to confront the restrictions posed by the system. Hence a central resource is to win legitimacy by gaining the support of society. To do this he engages in activities to win over supporters, possibly providing them with concrete benefits. A leader's popularity is a useful tool to convince detractors about the cost of changing the agenda. This does not necessarily require populist policies but it does call for action that has a high symbolic value for the population. The soft power usurper has more faith in his personal power than in political rules. If he can, he tends to go against the normative framework to accumulate power or ensure the permanency of his government. The soft power usurper always takes advantage of any favourable situation to weaken his opponents or to dominate press coverage. He is not worried about party control or the needs of the citizenry. The political party is merely a vehicle by which he achieves his aims. Soft power usurpers have no compunction about using resources to divide public opinion or insult their opponents. Democracy for the soft power usurper is most definitely a means not an end. This type of leader is a rule challenger, a soft polarizer and a power builder (Table 2.4).

In turn, power usurpers accumulate power by absorbing it from other state institutions, either by minimizing the role of the legislative or by undermining the independence of the judiciary. Power usurpers are democratic leaders since they have been elected in free elections. In some cases, they are very popular leaders, who have achieved more than 50 per cent of the vote. However, while democratically legitimate in origin, some end up manipulating constitutional or electoral instruments to increase personal power, thus worsening the

TABLE 2.4 The soft power usurper

Rule challenger	Sporadically manipulates constitutional or electoral instruments
	Sporadically usurps power from institutions
	Uses clientelism and populism to increase his personal power
	Undermines civil liberties and freedom of the press
	Undermines horizontal accountability
Soft polarizer	Accepts polarization
	Somewhat intolerant
	Avoids a power-sharing decision-making process
Power builder	Capacity to ignore the rules and citizens
	Attempts to undermine political opposition
	Ideologically strong
	Wish to perpetuate himself in government
	Accords more importance to personal promotion than to democracy

quality of democracy. Power usurpers can be part of a political party, but the party tends to be a mere tool to augment power or win elections. In many cases, the party has been created to support the leader or is manipulated to increase the leader's power. This type of leader does not accept power-sharing decision-making processes. They are autonomous and, by usurping power, they increase their capacity to ignore rules and citizens while in government. Power usurpers believe that they are the only legitimate representatives of their people. Politics becomes embedded in them. In Latin America, power usurpers usually establish populism and clientelism as political instruments to retain power. They tend to aspire to perpetuating themselves in power. They could be considered self-interested leaders or unethical leaders according to Aristotle and Kellerman, respectively. Power usurpers are prone to hard power. They are defined as rule manipulators, polarizers and power maximizers (Table 2.5).

TABLE 2.5 The power usurper

Rule manipulator	Manipulates constitutional or electoral instruments
	Usurps power from institutions
	Uses clientelism and populism to increase his personal power
	Undermines civil liberties and freedom of the press
	Undermines horizontal accountability
Polarizer	Increases the polarization of society
	Intolerant
	Does not accept a power-sharing decision-making process
Power maximizer	High capacity to ignore the rules and citizens
	Undermines political opposition
	Ideological polarization
	Perpetuates himself in government
	Accords more importance to personal promotion than to democracy

We do not offer this typology as an end explanation; rather its aim is to be a reliable tool to classify leaders and understand their impact on the quality of democracy.

Conclusion

When we developed our study, one of the main trends in Latin America was the deterioration of political parties with the reinforcement of presidentialism. Our typology reflects that. We have suggested four types of leaders and we describe them according to their relation with the rules (obey, challenge or manipulate), the opposition (polarize, tolerate or build consensus) and power (share, concentrate or usurp). We want to emphasize that the four types describe democratic leaders who have been elected by free and fair elections. Our typology advances the idea that they can became illegitimate owing to the way they subsequently exercise power.

In the following pages we use our typology to analyse leaders in each of our case studies. First, we examine the context, offering an analysis of the post-crises scenarios. Secondly, we lay out the qualitative analysis of the interviews. Finally, we examine case studies using our typology. Therefore what follows has two levels of analysis. First, we contextualize the understanding and the exercise of leadership at the national level. Secondly, we confront our typology with specific cases which were discussed in the interviews, such as Álvaro Uribe or Cristina Fernández de Kirchner.

As our study contextualizes leadership, we suggest that the emergence of different types of leader has to be explained by a combination of domestic conditions and individuals' ability, and therefore we combine these two different levels.

The next chapter shows how the combination of strong parties in different political contexts gave rise to distinct leaderships in Uruguay and Colombia.

CHAPTER 3

Leadership in the Context of a Stable Party System: Uruguay and Colombia

Introduction

In the second chapter we set out the different types of leadership in our typology, which we based on the arguments expressed by the politicians we interviewed. The two cases we discuss in this chapter both have stable political systems and strong political parties but went through very different crises. The political responses to these crises were also different. While in Uruguay the response followed the democracy enhancer leadership model, in Colombia we see the ambivalent democrat model.

According to the literature, political parties should have institutionalized mechanisms to control their leaders (Fabbrini 2009: 209; Valenzuela 2004: 5–19). This is indeed the case in both Uruguay and Colombia, but with different degrees of intensity. From the fifty-six interviews we carried out in Uruguay it was clear that the Uruguayan political class understood the historical context in which they were operating and could introduce new alternative policies without upsetting the institutional foundation of the country. Uruguay has a collective leadership rather than an individual one. It can interpret problems and find solutions without breaking with existing norms.

If there is a change of administration from one party to another, the leaders strengthen the democratic institutions and accept the limits imposed by legislation. They are politicians who stimulate political competition and do not seek to subjugate their opponents. Politics is based on responsibility and consensus-building. When in power, governments broaden the spectrum of rights and civil liberties and then step down without having changed the rules to their own benefit. The political race is considered to be a long, slow process with distinct stages. Their democratic leaders are not autonomous but work within an institutional framework that they strengthen and respect.

Colombia has had a stable exclusive two-party system. The Liberal Party (Partido Liberal, PLC) and the Conservative Party (Partido Conservador, PC) dominated the political scene from the middle of the nineteenth century until the end of the last century, when there was a degree of opening of the party system. This domination brought about personalist leaders and a concentration of power in them. However, the party system held firm. The division of powers also functions well. Following our fifty-four interviews we categorize the Colombian political class as being closest to the ambivalent democrat model. On a number of occasions there were attempts to change the legal framework but the institutions imposed limits on these reforms. Leaders respected state and party rules even though they did try to take more power for themselves. This led to a peculiar crisis situation. Unlike the economic and political imbalances in the other cases in our study, the Colombian crisis was the product of political violence and the break-up of the state's monopoly over security. Colombia has at times departed from democratic rules and then at others embraced them more fully. Our interviews in Colombia enabled us to observe how the different political forces interact and compete within a set framework of regulations. But it was also clear that the political game involves a degree of rather shady dealing and clientelist practices that erode the system.

This chapter analyses the different leadership types in Uruguay and Colombia. We first look at the political contexts, in particular the party political system in Uruguay and constitutional reform in Colombia. Secondly, we offer a detailed examination of our interviews, comparing the party systems with the types of leadership. Thirdly, using our leadership typology, we outline the types of leader that pertain to each country. The final section puts forward some ideas about the leadership types that emerge in stable party systems.

Contexts and systems at times of crisis

Uruguay

In the democracy index published in 2013 by the Economist Intelligence Unit (2013), Uruguay is the only country in South America to be considered a full democracy. The only other qualifying Latin American country in this group of twenty-six countries is Costa Rica. Chile is in thirty-fourth place. Then, farther down the list, starting with forty-sixth place, there are other countries from the region such as Panama, Brazil and Mexico. The index is based on five categories: electoral processes and pluralism, civil liberties, functioning of government, political participation and political culture. In the case of Uruguay, the categories of civil liberties and electoral processes and pluralism score 10, while political participation scores less than 5. Political culture scores 7.5 and the functioning of government 8.57. Obviously there are a few weaknesses in this index. Nonetheless, it is an instrument that shows something quite clear: Uruguay stands out as a positive beacon of democracy in the region. This is even clearer within the framework of our comparative study on political leadership.

The relative calm enjoyed by the Uruguayan political system hides dynamic innovative processes. Uruguay has a stable and pluralist party system with a culture of consensus rather than polarization

(Lanzaro 2001; Cason 2002). Pluralism is a long-standing characteristic that grew out of the balance of power between the different political forces. Although Uruguay is a country where politicians are well known by name, Uruguayan leaders such as Jorge Batlle, Julio María Sanguinetti, Luis Lacalle, Tabaré Vázquez and José Mujica did not personalize politics. They did not seek to concentrate power in their own hands or hold on to power indefinitely (Diamint and Tedesco 2014: 39).

The Argentine crisis in 2001 caused a lot of turbulence for the Uruguayan banking system. Uruguayan banks received a large number of deposits from Argentine citizens who were trying to escape the collapse of their economy. In 2002 some of the deposits began to be withdrawn, which risked the security of the Uruguayan banks. President Jorge Batlle of the Colorado Party decided to step in to bail out some of the banks but not others, thereby increasing uncertainty. The banking crisis and the situation in Argentina led to social unrest and looting. But the citizens did not demand 'all must go' (*que se vayan todos*). President Batlle ended his term in office with a very low approval rating but the party system did not disintegrate. At the end of his mandate in 2004, the Colorado Party had only ten deputies and three senators. Batlle won a seat in the Senate, heading the Colorado list, but he refused to take it, blaming himself for his party's defeat.

Uruguay had been a stable democracy from 1918 until it broke down in 1973 with the administration of President Juan María Bordaberry. He allowed a civil–military dictatorship to be installed, which lasted until 1985. Following the failure of a plebiscite in 1980, which the military hoped would legitimize their rule, a process was set in motion to achieve a consensus with civil society. To this end, the military sought the involvement of the political parties. The parties that were 'frozen' during the dictatorship were in a good position to rejoin political society once the political arena was reopened (Rial 1990: 24; González 1985). The Naval Club Pact led to an opening of politics with the inclusion of left-wing parties and their legalization. Although the armed forces tried to stonewall over the amnesty created in the pact, they did agree to allow the legalization of Frente Amplio.

These first elections brought Julio María Sanguinetti (1985–90), of the Colorado Party, to power. He had proved himself an able negotiator with the military, which agreed to step down peacefully. The National Party (known also as the Blancos) suffered a degree of fragmentation and division but began to reconstruct itself thanks to a young politician, Luis Alberto Lacalle (1990–95), and some alternative policies. During the presidency of Jorge Luis Batlle Ibáñez (2000–05), who came from a traditional political family, the country suffered the 2002 financial crisis. The devaluation of the peso and an increase in public debt had a definitive effect on the result of the presidential elections of 31 October 2004. Batlle's rival from five years previously, Tabaré Vázquez (2005–10) of the Frente Amplio, won the presidency.

The victory of Frente Amplio marked a fundamental change for the Uruguayan political system. As Lanzaro and De Armas said (2012: 3): 'the change – which is major but which takes place with state institutions and plurality intact and effective political competition – culminates with the victory of the Left in the 2004 elections, its entry into national government'. This profound transformation took place within the limits stipulated by democracy, the Constitution and Uruguayan law. Consequently, despite the crisis, the political system did not collapse, or even tremble a little. Instead it was strengthened. The arrival of Frente Amplio injected some dynamism into politics, which had previously been dominated by an old leadership and a small number of elites who essentially exchanged power periodically.

Some analysts maintain that a transition took place from a two-party system of the Blanco and Colorado parties to a two-party system between the Frente and the old political parties (De Armas 2010;

Luna 2007). While Gustavo de Armas considers the Frente to be a maverick party, other analysts, such as José Rilla (1999), believe it to be simply a new form of traditional party. Many academics agree that both the traditional two-party system and the new one which includes the Frente have created a political culture free of extremes. The system absorbs conflict and moderates disagreements (Buquet and Chasquetti 2005; González 1985).

This post-transition process demonstrated that democracy is fully embedded in the country and that crises can be resolved through institutional mechanisms. As Daniel Buquet (2000: 141) explains: 'the Uruguayan political system – very stable, institutionalized and consolidated in comparative terms – is also more complex than those in other countries in the region. The most complicating factor is the internal factionalism in Uruguayan political parties and the resulting difficulties this creates within the legislature.' The internal make-up of the political parties fosters rivalry in local committees. This creates a political system with many divisions and potential alliances. The factions within each party have their own conflicts and group loyalties. But there is no disloyalty, nobody changes party, nor is there any instability. Internal party disagreement does not spill over into institutions. Hence the establishment of a new party did not break the political system. There were some changes but continuity and respect for established rules prevailed. The presidents since the return to democracy have had different political ideologies but they have all been democracy enhancers.

Colombia

The Colombian political system is defined by contradictions: legitimacy and democratic stability coexist with extreme poverty, the absence of the state in rural areas, political violence, ideological intolerance, human rights violations and corruption. With an institutionalized party system, free elections and a political class with extensive experience in public policy, Colombia is surprising because it has maintained its democratic appearance while resorting to political violence.

When people talk about the Colombian political system, they tend to point out that the country has the oldest political parties in Latin America. In that respect it is similar to Uruguay. It also, like Uruguay, has a two-party system which arose in the middle of the nineteenth century. The Liberal (1848) and Conservative (1849) parties had an iron grip on power based on alternation. The Colombian political elite is an urban and provincial political class tied to concentrated economic power.[1]

Colombian politics is dominated by an elite composed of a few traditional families who essentially take it in turns to hold power. These traditional elites in both urban and rural areas are key to understanding how Colombia has maintained a degree of political stability within the context of a long civil war. In the words of one of the politicians we interviewed, 'these elites have managed to maintain order, the presence of the state and the economic development of the country where it mattered while ignoring the rest of the country as being rather unimportant in their bid to enrich themselves'.

The two traditional parties, the Liberals and Conservatives, had different characteristics at the beginning. The Liberals promoted liberty, free education, federalism, the separation of Church and state and universal suffrage. The Conservatives were in favour of strong unitary governments, a dominant position for the Church, centralism and restricted voting. Both parties have members from different social classes. They have set up a pragmatic alliance with the Frente Nacional, which allows them to alternate in power (Dávila Ladrón de Guevara 1997).

It is interesting to observe how even nowadays politics remains the preserve of the same families. This is clear from the words of a Liberal Party representative. He said he had forged his political career climbing each rung of the ladder. He claimed, 'I am not the son of a politician, I am not from a rich family, I am not a member of a political elite. I am simply a citizen who forged his own path.' However, farther on in the interview, it was revealed that his parents worked in politics, they were from a military family and that his grandfather was friends with the Liberal leader Jorge Eliécer Gaitán, who was assassinated in 1948. However, even those who do not consider themselves part of the old elite are still part of the traditional political class. To understand this elitism better, a note in the magazine *Semana* (2014) talked about the recent presidential elections in 2014 and stated that 'among genealogists in Colombia there is a tradition of finding out which of the presidential candidates is a descendant of the Ibáñez sisters'. They were two sisters at the time of independence who are famous not only for their beauty but also because one of them, Bernardina, was Simón Bolívar's lover, and the other, Nicolasa, was General Santander's lover. In the presidential elections of that year there were two descendants: the president, Juan Manuel Santos, and the Polo (PDA, Polo Democrático Alternivo) candidate, Clara López Obregón. This mark of origin drives home the point that Colombian politics is elitist.

Once the historical period known as '*La Violencia*'[2] was over, a phase of stability known as the National Front Regime (1958–74) began. Under this agreement, the two parties shared power, dividing up the posts in public administration and public corporations between themselves. According to some analyses this system became a single-party regime with no formal opposition but which was defined superficially as bi-party (Ramírez Huertas 2009: 32).

The regime was based on the exclusion of third political forces or new parties. There were some smaller parties such as the Colombian Communist Party (PCC), which was formed in 1930, and the Revolutionary Independent Labour Movement (MOIR), set up in 1969. These parties did not, however, achieve any parliamentary representation (Morales 1978: 56–73; Urrego Ardila 2013: 135–45).

This elitist exclusive political system led to depoliticization and abstention on the part of society. It is possible that this was a factor in encouraging the guerrilla movement to come into being. They demanded a more egalitarian and inclusive form of politics. That fictitious democratic legality forced opponents to operate outside the system. It is also worth remembering that Colombia not only has the oldest political parties in Latin America, it also has the oldest guerrilla movement in the region.

The 1991 constitutional process was an opportunity to increase political representation (Restrepo 2006). Nevertheless, the results were not very successful. According to some analysts, the reform did not bring about renewal but stagnation. Ramírez Huertas holds that after more than twelve years since the Colombian Constitution was promulgated, nothing had changed. He maintains that the new Constitution consolidated the lack of party discipline and electoral microenterprises (Ramírez Huertas 2009: 40–41). Other analysts claim that the Constitution promised reconciliation but that the 'political class was not renewed. It became corrupted, allied itself with new sectors or foreign interests to the detriment of the well-being of the community' (Semana 2011).

The fragmentation and volatility of electoral preferences have prompted analysts to characterize the party system as multiparty (Batlle and Puyana 2011: 27–57). In every election many parties are formed and then disbanded but put forward national and local lists of candidates. For example, the Democratic Alliance, which was made up of members of the former guerrilla movement M-19, was practically wiped out. Leaders, such as Noemí Sanín, who do gain some political space and who attract a high percentage of votes do not manage to create a party. Antanas Mockus, who was a professor and rector at the University of Colombia, went from being a much-praised manager, promoter of honest management and a citizens' culture for peace, to being a creator or candidate of various polit-ical groupings. In 2010 Mockus joined the Green Party and fought against Juan Manuel Santos in the second round. On 9 June 2011, Mockus left the Green Party and announced his retirement from politics.

There is another strange contradiction in Colombian politics between a country in the midst of guerrilla and paramilitary violence and one with consistently good economic growth indices. That economic development did not, however, lead to an increase in democracy: 'economic growth helped to reduce absolute poverty and to a lesser extent income inequality since the middle of the first decade of the twenty-first century. Nevertheless, Colombia is still one of the most unequal countries in the world' (Estudios Económicos de la OCDE 2013: 9; Bonilla González 2011: 46–65).

As the 1991 reform did not modernize the party system or restore popular faith in political representation it was necessary to introduce other changes. The demand for this was what brought Álvaro Uribe (2002–10) to power. The failure of previous presidents to solve the problem of the guerrillas opened up the game to a new type of leadership. The changes proposed by Uribe generated some doubts about democratic institutionality. There were suspicions that some judges were being tempted by hefty payments from the government to permit immediate re-election to be introduced. Congress approved a Political Reform in 2003. Thanks to this, President Uribe was re-elected in May 2006 with 62.2 per cent of the vote (Leal and Roll 2013; Durán Escalante 2006: 113–35). A crushing victory which did not provide for greater democratic access for the citizenry.

We could agree that since it came into being as a state, Colombia has had a democratic image which masks a different reality. Initially we classed Uruguay and Colombia as being similar cases. In both examples we see a system of democratic leadership. But the interviews told a different story. The dominant and exclusive party system allows for a kind of ambivalent democrat. The context enables new parties to emerge but they are ephemeral. They do not manage to survive three consecutive electoral contests. Rodríguez Rincón defines this harshly as: 'we are not in the presence of real parties but electoral microenterprises which brandish improbable party banners' (Rodríguez Rincón 2006). Based on the interviews we carried out for our five case studies, we suggest that the party system and its degree of institutionalization are crucial to the emergence of different types of leadership. We argue that a fragmented, exclusive party system does not generate democratic leadership. Colombia helps to structure this argument.

Party systems and types of leadership

Uruguay

Both the party system and access to power in Uruguay involve clear rules which have helped to ensure well-defined political careers (Botinelli 2008). Leaders begin their political careers at local level as *ediles*. The next step along the road is to enter Congress as an alternate deputy. Some end up being senators, which is considered the peak of their political career. In Uruguay senators are most definitely considered the political elite (ibid.). This structured and long career is what explains how old the politicians are. In the interviews, time and again we were told that a leader of fifty-five years of age is considered young in Uruguayan politics. Seventy-one per cent of the political leaders we interviewed owed their positions to having worked their way up the echelons of their political party.

In Uruguay, the vast majority of politicians stay in the same party for their entire life. An academic we interviewed summarized the relationship between politicians and their parties: 'in Uruguay *outsiders* are *insiders*, you cannot be a pure *outsider* within this system; you have to go through party channels'. Staying in one party and the stability of the political careers have strengthened a political class which had to manage the transition to and consolidation of democracy. It is an educated and engaged elite. Some 45 per cent of those interviewed have a university degree and 40 per cent also have a postgraduate qualification.

Political parties have been vital actors in the formation of the Uruguayan state. In the words of one interviewee: 'the traditional parties as a political administrative structure came before the state but also pre-dated the constitution of the Uruguayan nationality ... the parties are central to the formation of our identity'. The coexistence of the political parties and their role in public administration have led to a politics of consensus, cooperation between the Blancos and the Colorados and institutional stability (Rilla 1999).

The arrival of the Frente Amplio heralded change but without any need to abolish the traditional parties or destroy existing rules. The Frente also breathed new life into the elite. According to available data, the left-wing parliamentarians are more diverse in terms of gender and professions linked to the social and human sciences. There is also a greater proportion of working people and trade union members (Serna 2005).

One of the Frente leaders defined it as being 'a political and programmatic agreement rather than ideology, which has helped to preserve the identity of each of the individual members'. Party membership is very important in Uruguay as a means of entering politics. Some 45 per cent of those we interviewed were party members, family tradition accounted for 26 per cent, and involvement in student politics accounted for 23 per cent.

The political parties are central to political life as the basis of policy-making and for promoting ideas and strategies. Politics still has local support bases and the party is also a sort of social club. One Blanco party deputy explained Uruguayan politics to us like this: 'Uruguay is not a country of extremes but averages. It is not a country of definite colours but of shades of colour. We do not like harsh words or taking risks. The state has the role of protector to play. In addition we have codes in Uruguay which keep everything in check. We never stop talking to each other in Uruguay.' This concept of politics made it possible to open up the political game and manage the leftover Blancos and Colorados.

In addition, Uruguayan society believes in democracy. In a study on the public image of legislative power, 73 per cent of those surveyed agreed with the phrase 'without political parties there could be no democracy' and 77 per cent agreed that 'without parliament there could be no democracy' (Buquet 2014: 3).

Their leaders respect the laws. President Tabaré Vázquez, despite belonging to a new party, did not change the rules of the game but actually consolidated the political system. Garcé (2010: 500–501) comments that 'Vázquez managed to achieve unparalleled levels of popularity and approval for his administration'. Garcé attributes this popularity to three facts: 'He made use of three things at his disposal: accountability, trips abroad and inaugurating public works' (ibid.: 501). The country continued unchanged even when in 2009 an ex-guerrilla, José Mujica, won the election. Garcé gives this explanation: 'the first steps in Presidente José Mujica's term confirm the "party-centric hypothesis": in Uruguay people don't govern, parties do' (ibid.: 530). All the points made by our interviewees conform to the model of democracy enhancer. There is no dissent between the three Uruguayan parties: in Uruguay there is a stable predictable political system.

We were very interested to hear time and again the word 'learning' from our interviewees. One female senator told us how during her years in prison she had the opportunity to think and learn. This helped her to understand how a 'Uruguayan citizen in the 1980s was very different from one in the 1970s'. She also maintained that 'we learn the most important political lessons from defeat'. This predisposition to learning, self-criticism and historical analysis is not to be found in our interviews with Argentines, Ecuadoreans or Venezuelans. The Frente and their politicians learned from past experience and pushed for change to ensure that they could represent voters in a relevant manner. José Mujica, who was spoken to about his guerrilla past, also talked of learning when he said: 'To some people I represent the 1970s when the world was very much bipolar. We have learned that in the game of liberal democracy we can do a great deal. We do not have the right to sacrifice one or two generations in the name of utopias' (Danza and Tulbovitz 2015: 66).

Our interviewees agreed that clientelism exists. The type that exists in Uruguay is what we call vertical clientelism, which is that between politicians and political supporters. Around 62 per cent of the interviewees identified clientelism as the exchange of benefits for votes. In the main these benefits are offering jobs to the party faithful or members of the party. The word clientelism was largely used in connection with political parties during the interviews: 'for many years citizens demanded jobs from the state owing to the lack of other employment. And that is what encouraged clientelism.' In the interviews many of the politicians explained clientelism as a party political instrument which is falling into disuse since the introduction of technology into public affairs is increasing transparency and competition when it comes to employment. Most of the interviewees considered clientelism as a necessary evil and something that will be difficult to eradicate. Most Uruguayan leaders (66 per cent) consider that clientelism is linked to the political culture and functions as a means of domination. The fundamental difference with countries such as Argentina, Ecuador or Venezuela is that clientelism does not seem to be used as a tool to increase personal power. Clientelism was actually described as a party policy that benefited members and supporters once their party had come to power. In our meetings, however, it was clear that the interviewees considered clientelism to be a problem for each of the three main parties in Uruguay.

The case of Uruguay was crucial for this study. Uruguay is very different from Argentina, Ecuador and Venezuela. The stable institutionalized party system, free and fair elections and a deep-rooted democratic political culture combine to produce democratic leaders. By contrast, party systems with a low degree of institutionalization or a high degree of autonomy (Argentina and Ecuador, and Venezuela, respectively) encourage power usurpers to come to the fore. Our qualitative analysis of the interviews carried out in Uruguay demonstrates that the extent to which the party system is institutionalized is the most significant variable in determining leader type. Uruguayan political parties are key to guarding against concentration of power. In addition, leaders are considered to be citizens. One Colorado deputy explained this very clearly: 'there is daily contact with politicians in Uruguay. You can go for a coffee and see Mujica [the president] at the next table having coffee with his wife or a friend. And he is the president of the republic. You can see ministers playing football and you can just sit down and watch. A while ago a report was published about whether legislators used bodyguards and it had not occurred to any of them to use them. I think that is good. We also do not have guards on legislative buildings here.' Although the country has had some very important leaders who have had a profound effect on its history, Uruguay has managed to avoid power usurpers. Under its two presidents, the Frente Amplio improved social conditions, carried out a tax reform and brought about a twenty-four-point fall in unemployment. The popularity of both leaders – Vázquez and Mujica – did not translate into any change in the electoral system.

The post-crisis scenario did not provoke any breaking of the rules. In the case of Uruguay it was the citizens who, when faced with the 2002 economic crisis, channelled their demands through the party system. The winning party, Frente Amplio, did not resort to weakening the opposition. Our interviewees maintained that this stability was not the result of strong or charismatic leaders but rather of trust in the democratic system and the strength of the political parties.

Colombia

The Colombian study also demonstrates the importance of political parties. However, as was to be expected, the interviews focused largely on the topics of political violence and corruption. The crisis in Colombia is one of global governability of its territory. Colombia has two faces. The judicial system seems to function and many corrupt politicians go to prison. But prison does not seem to be a deterrent. Even if they spend a few years in prison, their family can carry on in politics on their behalf. The stolen money is not recovered. Hence while the justice system might well pursue the corrupt, the arrogance of the political class explains just how little they are dissuaded from wrongdoing by the threat of punishment or even imprisonment. The combination of political violence and an efficient justice system that actually does not really deter crime means that there is no such thing as democratic order in Colombia.

Some writers suggest that Colombians are used to sectarian and not very democratic politics. Pizarro explains that 'in Colombia there is no culture of democratic opposition. Neither the one-party hegemonic governments of the past nor the Frente Nacional provided fertile ground for that culture to flourish' (Pizarro Leongómez 1996: 218–19). However, this does not fully explain the political careers of the presidents. For example, Andrés Pastrana Arango, Uribe's predecessor, had a stellar career in politics using the tools of democracy. He was part of the traditional political elite since his father, Misael Pastrana Borrero, had been president of the republic between 1970 and 1974 and leader of the Colombian Conservative Party. His son was the first mayor of Bogotá to be elected by popular vote (1988–90). Then he was a senator of the republic. In 1998 he was elected president with 51 per cent of the vote, defeating the Liberal candidate, Horacio Serpa.

Pastrana was responsible for negotiating the Colombia Plan with the United States, which provided financial support to the

Colombian government to help counteract the insurgency in exchange for efforts to fight drug production and trafficking. Of the total, 51 per cent of the resources were destined to support programmes to improve social conditions and respect for human rights and strengthen state institutions. The efforts to fight the guerrillas were to run in parallel with democratic strengthening. However, the Colombia Plan really focused on combating drug trafficking and fighting the Revolutionary Armed Forces of Colombia (Fuerzas Armadas Revolucionarias de Colombia, FARC), and so had a heavy military component. With the arrival of Uribe in the presidency, this repressive aspect intensified. At the start of 2002 Pastrana considered his strategy to have failed and suspended the peace process with the FARC. His party was decimated in the elections. Uribe capitalized on the discontent, placing the breakdown in the peace negotiations at the heart of his campaign.

His predecessor, Ernesto Samper, was elected in the Liberal Party primaries, meaning that his presidential candidacy had come about as a result of following democratic procedures. But he was accused of accepting a large campaign donation from drug traffickers. Under his government violence escalated both among common criminals and the far-right paramilitary organizations, the Self-Defence Units of Colombia (Autodefensas Unidas de Colombia, AUC), and the left-wing guerrillas.

We can, therefore, observe the existence of institutionalized political careers but which have some characteristics that are more common in uninstitutionalized systems. Cárdenas Ruiz points out three current trends in Colombian politics: the rise of personalist governments, disaffection with parties and lack of ideological identity. 'Faced with the question "describe with one word what politics means to you" 33 per cent of those surveyed associated it with corruption, 10 per cent with injustice, 9 per cent with democracy, 5 per cent with the common good, and 18 per cent did not know how to describe it' (Cárdenas Ruiz 2012). This dominance of corruption as a political evil is substantiated also by a LAPOP study: 'It is worth pointing out that in 2012 Colombia was ranked first among the countries for the level of perception of corruption, with an average of 82 points on a scale of 0 to 100' (Rodríguez Raga and Seligson 2012: 95, 206).

All of these characteristics help to explain the emergence of a leader such as Álvaro Uribe, who combined authoritarianism with popularity. Uribe stands out in the Colombian context as a soft power usurper – a type of usurpation supported by a large majority who are not interested in 'the rule of law, constitutional guarantees, judicial process, democratic institutions, checks and balances as laid out in the 1991 Constitution, national or international laws' (Mejía Quintana 2009). Despite his rather different ideological leaning, Álvaro Uribe, like Rafael Correa in Ecuador, Hugo Chávez in Venezuela or Cristina Fernández de Kirchner in Argentina, mobilized his supporters and had a fixed logic of friends/enemies. The majority of those interviewed from the opposition party, the Alternative Democratic Pole (Polo Democrático Alternativo), were convinced that the Uribe coalition government was controlled by para-politicians, rural and urban leaders linked to the paramilitary organizations. However, Uribe's high level of popularity and speeches about defeating the guerrillas were not enough to win him a third victory. His leadership did eventually come up against the relative autonomy of the state institutions, which defended democracy and limited his ability to concentrate power in his hands.

For its part, the leadership of Juan Manuel Santos had more in common with that of the more traditional leaders in Colombia. His approach demonstrated that Colombia had maintained the tradition of ambivalent democrat. Santos is conciliatory and he seeks consensus. Santos also has the media on his side by virtue of his family. He is a president who returned to democratic legality. Santos also began a concerted effort to negotiate with the FARC.

One possible explanation as to why the electorate switched preferences from Uribe to Santos is that although Uribe managed to re-establish a degree of public order, he did so in rather illegitimate ways. Having achieved a degree of order, society then preferred a candidate who would reinstate democratic rules. Although President Santos corrected a lot of his predecessor's 'deviations', he did not focus on improving the political system, reforming party finance or reducing clientelism.

In the following section we are going to examine these differences through the lens of our leadership typology. The information gained from our interviews provides key data to achieve this.

The profile of leadership

Uruguay

We argue that in Uruguay leaders are democratic enhancers. The interviews revealed a model of leadership which matches our description of Uruguay as a rule developer, a bridge builder and respectful of democracy (see Table 2.2).

Rule developer

Our interviews in Uruguay revealed just how important respect for the rule of law is in that country. Hence leadership is considered to be a support for and promoter of democratic institutions, horizontal accountability and civil rights and liberties. One opposition legislator said that 'when a law has the support of all the parties, it is symbolically as well as formally stronger'. Laws are so important that a Colorado leader said that 'we have to prioritize the defence of democratic values and the rule of law'. Leaders aim to promote civil rights and freedoms.

In Uruguay party activism is politics. Some 71 per cent of the politicians we interviewed got their jobs thanks to having worked in their political parties. This does not mean there is an absence of trade union or student activism but rather that leadership largely emerges from political parties. The party system is stable. The bi-party system broke down but the Frente Amplio injected new life into the political system, strengthening the institutions.

Control over the leaders is carried out at all levels. Society holds them to account in the party conferences, in which citizens can question their representatives. Their peers hold them to account; as one Frente Amplio deputy said: 'we have an important degree of social control here, we have a small population and actually we all know each other so there is a degree of social control whereby anybody who shows off is told off'. Another deputy also said that the opposition exerts a degree of control over leaders: 'I spend a lot of my time monitoring things, asking for reports, calling ministers.'

President Tabaré Vázquez implemented the 'Democratic Uruguay' programme, the main idea of which was to make public administration more transparent and to open up political power to civil society. The main instrument to achieve this was the Strategy for Fostering Citizen Participation. Meanwhile, President Mujica donated his presidential salary to the poor. Mujica said: 'We know these things won't change the world but we increase our commitment to society. This is a moral and ethical obligation' (FM Centro 2015).

One opposition deputy stressed how actually a concentration of power frightens the Uruguayan political class: 'the only problem with democracy is that sometimes a party can win over 50 per cent of the vote. Then democracy, which is essentially political freedom, the majority governing, can lose respect for minorities. Then we stop being a democracy and we start to get used to things that are rather more at home in dictatorial regimes. Then we do not have the liberal game that needs majorities and minorities to find solutions.'

Political leadership in Uruguay is understood from the perspective of respect for institutions and the promotion of the rule of law. Fifty-eight per cent of our interviewees maintained that the main function of democracy is to guarantee the division of powers.

In the Uruguayan interviews, the leaders interpreted leadership as a collective issue. The parties and institutions of the state are a fundamental pillar of political leaderships.

Bridge builder

All the interviews in Montevideo emphasized the importance of political consensus. Political competition in Uruguay is not a zero-sum game. One Blanco deputy said that 'political activity is largely about negotiation, articulation and consensus'. President Mujica himself also stressed this idea. He said that his presidency would be a question of 'negotiate, negotiate, negotiate until it is unbearable' (El País 2009).

One of the interviewees explained that reaching consensus with the opposition is important but 'consensus without losing your identity. We have to be careful otherwise people will think we are all the same. We have different ideologies and a different vision for the country.' Political consensus is valued given the differences that separate the parties.

Uruguayan leaders understand politics as responsibility. As a leader of Frente Amplio said: 'there is no need for consensus but there is a need for compromise'. That compromise, as an ex-minister from Frente Amplio said, is what binds together the policies of state: 'I believe we created a consciousness within the Uruguayan political system of the need to seek and articulate agreement, with the broadest possible support, and approved by the political system as a whole'. Another interviewee said that 'the magic of Uruguay is that nobody can crush anybody'.

A Colorado deputy expressed similar ideas: 'The democratic system is the best because it makes for consensus. We have a non-confrontational style. You can have strong convictions but still respect the other person's point of view. We also respect those who behave differently since none of us can claim to be the masters of truth.' This idea of consensus-building and respect for others seems to be a quality shared by all members of the Uruguayan political class.

The inclination to share power was very clear from the ideas about accepting the limits of the governing party. An important member of Frente Amplio said: 'Frente Amplio accepted that only half the population voted for us. There is another half which did not support us and we have to consider them too. There is a good relationship between the different parties. It is a shared collective vision, shared although there are a few social issues on which we disagree (such as abortion and euthanasia)'.

A well-known political scientist explained this collective vision: 'even when the leader is very important such as Tabaré or Mujica, they are still leaders of parties, groups and sectors. They are still connected and can be voted down. That to me is a key point about democracy that nobody is above everything.' Power for Uruguayan leaders is not a personal attribute. It is a joint project with the community. Consensus-building and tolerance are natural attributes for Uruguayan political leaders.

This tradition will probably continue under Tabaré Vázquez, who took office in March 2015. Vázquez said that in government he will hold a dialogue with all political forces. In his victory speech on being elected he said: 'We can celebrate a climate of peace, respect, and republican sentiment today. It is our nation's way of being an achievement for all Uruguayans' (El País 2014). To understand this dominant democratic climate in Uruguay, it is worth listening to the eloquence of his opponent at the ballot box: 'the results will be praised, respected and defended. We are not supporters of majorities who make mistakes but majorities who lead' (ibid.). Both candidates show great tolerance.

Vázquez won in the second round of voting with 53.6 per cent of the vote. This was the largest victory in a second round since the current electoral system was introduced in 1996. Tabaré Vázquez became the president to garner the most votes in the last seventy years. Luis Lacalle Pou, his rival, won 41.1 per cent of the vote. One conclusion from the 2014 elections is that 'apart from the numbers, Uruguay deepened the democratic values that have characterized the government since the return to democracy in 1986: whoever governs respects the institutions of the republic and the democratic rules of the game' (ibid.). These conclusions back up our depiction of Uruguayan leaders as democracy enhancers.

Respectful

The characteristic that defines Uruguay and sets it apart from its neighbours is that it is political parties rather than individuals which lead the country. The political parties provide an identity to a group, understand their situation, set an agenda and propose solutions. In the Uruguayan context the party is the necessary channel for mediation (Garcé 2009: 110). A Frente Amplio senator described this enthusiastically: 'in Uruguay party loyalty is important for everything, but people do it with pride, Blancos, Colorados and Frenteamplista. The people also do it with pride and respect each other.'

There is a party system and fixed rules of the political game. As a Blanco party leader said, 'governability is high in this country because of the strength of the institutions'. Uruguayan politicians do not break the rules or change the constitution. They do not pass laws to benefit themselves personally. A Frente Amplio deputy stated very clearly: 'the candidate is nothing more than an instrument by which to express the ideas of the political party but alone they cannot govern'.

This idea also comes over in President Mujica's evaluation: 'I would have liked to have done more but at least I tried to convey a very republican image, to drive home the fact that nobody is better than anybody else and that the president is just like any other member of society, that he is not above the people and that morally I have been loyal to the interests of the country' (El Espectador 2014).

An analysis of the changes to the *Ley de Caducidad* proposed by Vázquez and Mujica exemplifies this devotion to the law. When Vázquez discovered, in October 2005, that the law did not apply to fifty cases of clandestine removal and forced disappearances of Uruguayan citizens, he saw a way of advancing human rights policy but without going against the law. He held a plebiscite on 25 October 2009, on the day of the election. The Supreme Court, in a unanimous judgement, declared that Articles 1, 3 and 4 of the *Ley de Caducidad* were unconstitutional. Six days later, once José Mujica had won the election, the Uruguayan electorate voted that the constitutional amendment would make part of the *Ley de Caducidad* invalid. The votes in favour of the measure averaged 48 per cent, but over 50 per cent was required for it to pass. As a result there was no reform and the *Ley de Caducidad* remained unchanged. Neither Vázquez nor Mujica tried to force the issue to achieve their objective.

In Uruguay institutions are respected: 'when a party comes to power its head, its president, becomes the president of all Uruguayans. This is also what brings about large governing coalitions,' explained a Colorado deputy. 'In Uruguay we know the limits of power. And we all respect them.'

Analysis of the interviews carried out in Uruguay helped to formulate our argument. Domestic political conditions and especially the degree of institutionalization of political parties are an important variable in explaining different types of leadership.

Colombia

Classifying leadership in Colombia was very difficult since it combines democratic elements with a very specific reality: violence. A well-known lawyer explained that there are formally democratic institutions in Colombia but taken as a whole they are very far from being democratic: 'Colombia has a democratic side and a violent side. This ambiguity is most obvious when you consider that the legal system coexists with a permanent state of exception.' The country is criss-crossed by serious structural violence. This was also remarked upon by a senator from the Alternative Democratic Pole (Polo Democrático Alternativo): 'in Colombia violence makes the political struggle very hard. Here nobody gives up their armoured cars, nobody. I have two armoured cars and five escorts which I consider normal. If you see the statistics you will see that every day a mayor is killed, somebody is kidnapped. In a nutshell, the Colombian state is a long way from having the monopoly over weapons. There are very powerful armed organizations on all sides.'

In Colombia we carried out interviews just after the start of Juan Manuel Santos' first term in office. Many of our interviewees commented on the differences in leadership style between Santos and Uribe (see Table 2.3).

Rule-obedient

Colombia has a democratic creed. There is a widespread belief among the political class that it is a democratic country. Several interviewees mentioned the importance of the rule of law to the Colombian political community.

Presidents have respected the freedom of the press. This has been under threat because of the state of violence in the country. For example, Andrés Pastrana agreed to a request from the Secretariat of the Inter-American Press (Secretaría Interamericana de Prensa, SIP) for clear instructions to be given to members of the security forces. They asked that journalists in conflict zones not be considered as military targets and that they not be subjected to any threats or intimidation (El Tiempo 2000). Pastrana explained his decision, saying: 'as a leader I understand and agree with the overriding principle that people who hold political power should respect freedom to inform and be informed as the best counterweight to power'.

President Santos has mentioned on several occasions the importance of safeguarding press freedom: 'freedom of the press, freedom of expression, the right to criticize, the right to demonstrate for or against something or some government is the essence of democracy. That is why I have always defended that right clearly and wholeheartedly' (Presidencia de la República 2013). He also agreed to open up the negotiations with the FARC in Cuba following criticism that they were taking place in secret. Our interviewees agreed that Santos did not have any problems with the media.

Many of our respondents suggested that political parties should not be overly conditioned by current events but rather should have a degree of ideological cohesion and long-term plan for the country. In the words of one deputy: 'a strong party, with an ideology, is very important for democracy. It is the fundamental basis for democracy.' When asked 'what is the role of political parties?' 52 per cent of the interviewees chose the option 'to structure the democratic game'.

In Colombia, as in Uruguay, we found traditional political parties. But in the case of Colombia these parties coexist with new organizations and their leaders often switch party. For example, President Juan Manuel Santos is the leader of the U party (Partido Social de Unidad Nacional), set up by Álvaro Uribe in 2005. Before that Santos was a member of the Liberal Party. For his part, Uribe was elected senator in the most recent elections in 2014 for the Democratic Centre (Centro Democrático). Leaders and parties seem to be quite flexible. A Liberal Party senator mentioned that 'parties are blooming in Colombia, I myself set up two because it was really easy to get 30,000 signatures'. However, political parties do not have the degree of coherence they had prior to 1991.

One of our interviewees claimed that most Colombian leaders do not take apart or build the democratic state but they do accept the rules of the game, even political violence. One representative of the Green Party said that 'nearly all the congressional presidents in the last ten years have been investigated by the Supreme Court and are in jail'. There is a permanent tension between corruption and the limits imposed by institutions. But as the Green Party representative explained, this illegality is part of Colombian culture, and although many congressmen end up in prison, 'several of them have their wives in Congress; they are in prison and their wives are in Congress with exactly the same votes that they won themselves'.

Receptive

Ambivalent democrats seek to build consensus by working on occasion with the opposition. In Colombia there is an old tradition of inter-party agreements. For example, in 2002, President Pastrana had organized the Common Front for Peace Multi-party Commission (Comisión Pluripartidaria del Frente Común por la Paz). He had also arranged a referendum on changes to the political system, inviting the opposition to lead the 'no' campaign.

In part as a consequence of the ongoing war, recent Colombian history has seen a host of multiparty initiatives to try to bring about peace. This is one of the characteristics that most of our interviewees see in President Santos. He asked the opposition to unite to work for peace and to reach an agreement with Venezuela. As a U senator commented, 'Santos is a great negotiator. He is a strategist. He is a man who likes building large coalitions. He is the heir to a tradition of political parties and mediation. He has the media, institutions and financial institutions on his side.' A social leader added that Santos 'up to now has maintained the independence and division of power, the system of checks and balances that exists in a liberal democracy.' According to most of our interviewees, Santos wants to share power.

The political party system in Colombia has historically not promoted polarization. According to one of our interviewees, the polarization engendered by Álvaro Uribe can be considered an exception. There is openness and tolerance but they do not necessarily translate into a broadening of democracy. In sum, this particular combination of exclusion and violence on one hand and tolerance, consensus and traditionalism on the other creates a pragmatic and little-ideologized power play.

Between soft challenger and power builder

The ambivalent democrat is a soft challenger. They are leaders who seek to accumulate personal power. In this process it is likely that they will seek to defy institutional power. However, they appreciate their limits and tend to agree to include their opponents. The leader accepts the law but tries to favour his own position. Unlike democracy enhancers, they respect but do not strengthen democracy. In the case of Colombia, the best example of this is Álvaro Uribe. Uribe oscillated between defying and accepting institutional rules. In our categorization Uribe can be considered a leader who unites the characteristics of ambivalent democrat and soft power usurper (see Table 2.4).

The Colombian institutions were able to put limits on some of Uribe's excesses, particularly his desire to stand for re-election after two consecutive terms. However, he did exploit his favourable situation to weaken his opponents and dominate press coverage. He did not hold back from using a number of resources to divide public opinion and insult his opponents. He created the National Social Unity Party or U party, which served as a vehicle to further his own personal aims. However, he was unable to limit the power of the Colombian state institutions and finally accepted the Electoral Court's decision that denied his request for constitutional reform to enable him to seek a third mandate.

According to some legislators we interviewed, Uribe was actually a product of the Colombian political system. The rise of Uribe can be interpreted as a consequence of specific political conditions. The crisis of representation of the political parties and civil weariness with the violence seem to have created the favourable conditions necessary for Uribe to win the elections.

Uribe achieved a special combination of efficiency and populism. From our perspective, the way he exercised power involved a manipulation of state institutions, the media and his party. For example, a report in the *Washington Post* stated that North American money, equipment and training for elite Colombian intelligence units to help combat drug trafficking were used to carry out undercover operations and campaigns to discredit the Supreme Court, and members of the opposition and civil society groups (DeYoung et al. 2011).

Uribe was very tough with the guerrillas and both his repressive Democratic Security Policy (Política de Seguridad Democrática) as well as the matter of 'false positives'[3] defied existing laws. Finally, the 2003 Anti-Terrorist Law broke a number of national treaties. It was strongly criticized by opposition congressmen and NGOs, who demanded that the armed forces be stripped of their judicial role.

Society as a whole went along with these methods and Álvaro Uribe enjoyed a lot of popularity. Despite reports that linked Uribe with the paramilitaries, his repressive security programme brought a degree of calm to the population. Operations of doubtful legality succeeded in reducing the power of the FARC. Uribe's real aim was to achieve a greater degree of security for the citizenry. He did this by accumulating power and weakening the existing bi-party system. Tackling inequality and building a new party system were not on his agenda (Galindo Hernández 2007: 148, 152).

Despite all these excesses, a Liberal senator we interviewed pointed out that 'nine members of the Constitutional Court said no to re-election and nothing happened, nobody shed a tear, nobody went out to demonstrate in Bolívar Square'. Even a young leader from the U party recognized that 'our great attachment to the rule of law came about because there is an institutional culture so it was possible to stop Álvaro Uribe by institutional means'. That led us to agree that Uribe is a leader who combines characteristics from both models.

Uribe exploited his position of popularity with the electorate to cut away at the power of his opponents. A Liberal Party senator told us, 'Uribe is a clear leader but polarized the country.' As we characterized in our leader typology, soft power usurpers use polarization as a means of asserting their leadership.

The answer to why the population did not react when confronted by an authoritarian leader seems to be clientelism. A Green Party leader commented, for example, that 'Boyacá in particular is a department with a very strong political tradition. It is a department where you can buy peasants with meat, beer and bricks.' Sixty-nine per cent of our interviewees said that people expect clientelism so it carries on. One deputy admitted that 'politicians generate a need among society to keep asking for things'.

A senator from the Liberal Party talked about clientelist skills: 'The electoral process is corrupt here. The merits of the candidates are not important, the only thing that matters is money and you can buy leaders of all sizes.' Uribe's success is attributable to the problem of violence, if we consider the argument put forward by one important bureaucrat in the executive: 'It is very difficult to achieve any form of democratic consolidation in a country in the middle of the type of violence we face, violence that threatens the freedom and peace of the population.' His charisma also had something to do with his popularity. Uribe captivated the population. He was also very intransigent with the opposition parties but did not wipe them out. He taunted them in ways that were more appropriate to street brawls than political debate.

A female senator from the U party admitted that the party was made up of people representing a range of ideas. The party did not have a clear identity nor the organizational tradition of the Liberal or Conservative parties. The party was seen as a vehicle for consolidating the Uribe project. The Uribe slogan 'Firm hand, big heart' struck a chord with voters who wanted peace. Uribe's response was to try to destroy the FARC. Hence he introduced the Democratic Security Policy. Ideologically it was nothing more than strongarm tactics. It worked. It restored confidence on the part of ordinary Colombians and won their support by using concrete decisions to resolve long-standing conflicts. Disillusionment turned to hope. However, it was along this road that Uribe let slip his democratic principles, but the population was not worried. What mattered was ending the violence. This is why the period of Álvaro Uribe has been described as authoritarian modernization (Rodríguez Garavito 2005: 14; Rodríguez Rincón 2006: 73). The president peddled hope and abused his position to gain results. This led to an increase in his power, which is why he is considered a power builder.

It is important to remember, though, that press freedom was not curtailed. Even a U party leader commented: 'the anti-Uribe criticism in Colombia was thanks to the fact that the media was free to express its views'. We see this combination again in the case of respect for civil rights, even though some practices went against established democratic rules.

The use of nationalist rhetoric, patriotic symbols and repression through the Democratic Security Policy all validated his strategy. But he could not remain in power. Uribe did not manage to become a power usurper. Despite the political violence in Colombia, the strength of the institutions and the degree of institutionalization of the political parties constrained a leader who swung from being an ambivalent democrat to a soft power usurper.

After Uribe's time in office, Santos restored the political style that had been the norm before. Colombian political tradition is a peculiar combination of clientelism, party disobedience, electoral microenterprises, corruption and factional organization, according to Ramírez Huertas (2009: 29). Santos did not confront the institutions but neither did he strengthen them.

Colombia has faced challenges to its institutions and rule of law. It is a country with territorial and institutional vacuums but it maintains a democratic appearance. But this is not a full democracy. In our interviews in Bogotá debate about the differences between Santos and Uribe was crucial. In our model, Santos is rule-obedient and Uribe a rule challenger. Several interviewees agreed that Juan Manuel Santos reinstated the country's best liberal traditions, which had been broken by Álvaro Uribe.

Conclusion

The case of Uruguay indicates that the degree of institutionalization of the political party system is a crucial element in understanding the emergence of different types of leader.

The interviews in Colombia show a political scenario that combines, paradoxically, stability and political violence. While the political party system seems to be institutionalized, political violence can be considered an excuse for the emergence of power usurpers. Indeed, Álvaro Uribe used the problem of political violence to attempt to increase his power. He was only partially successful. Despite political violence, the institutions in Colombia were able to block the emergence of a power usurper.

Is a stable party system a condition for excluding power usurpers? Uruguay and Colombia seem to suggest this conclusion. Therefore, collapse or fragmentation of a party system could increase the possibilities for the emergence of power usurpers. The following cases, Argentina and Ecuador, witnessed the deterioration of their party systems after deep economic crisis. We now apply our typology to politically unstable contexts to be able to answer the following questions: Does the degree of institutionalization of the party system make a difference with regard to different types of leader? Is our typology appropriate to explain leaders in Argentina and Ecuador? Are post-crisis scenarios fertile times for democracy enhancers or power usurpers?

As in this chapter, we present the following cases in two levels of analysis – analysis of the political context and of individual leaders.

CHAPTER 4

Leadership in the Context of a Crisis: Argentina and Ecuador

Introduction

Argentina and Ecuador underwent economic and political crises at the beginning of the 2000s. In each case the post-crisis scenario was dominated by the emergence of strong political leaders who have been able to achieve economic and political stabilization. In this chapter, we present an analysis of political leadership in those two countries. It is based on the results of 118 interviews in Buenos Aires and Quito[1] with legislators, former presidents, former vice-presidents and party leaders. They discussed with us the post-crisis scenarios, the fall and rise of different political leaders, the role of the political parties and the main features of the new political leaders.

This chapter starts by analysing the 2001 crisis in Argentina. It briefly explores different leadership models that emerged before and after the crisis. The second section studies the long crisis that Ecuador faced from 1995. The section suggests some ideas about the emergence of Rafael Correa. The third section offers an analysis of the post-crisis scenario in both countries. The fourth section presents the conceptualization of political leaders in Argentina and

Ecuador. This is based on qualitative analysis of the interviews undertaken in Buenos Aires and Quito. It considers our typology of leaders and examines different examples from both countries. The conclusion offers some ideas about the political conditions that prompt the emergence of different types of leader.

The reasons for the crises

Between December 2001 and January 2002, politically and economically Argentina came to a standstill. In 2001, Argentinian president Fernando de la Rúa was forced to resign, owing to his inability to rescue the economy from a deep and long recession. The slogan chanted in the streets was *que se vayan todos* ('all must go'). However, the political crisis was resolved by the old elite that still dominated the political landscape: the Peronist Party, created in 1945, and the Radical Party, formed in 1890.

An economic recession began in 1994 with the Mexican crisis and deepened in 1998 after Brazil's devaluation, bringing to an end a period of economic growth and stability that had started in 1991. In his second term in office Carlos Menem was unable to adjust the economic strategy to the recession and increased the external and internal public debt. The convertibility plan became a straitjacket that prevented the government devaluing to regain international competitiveness (Tedesco 2002; Corrales 2002). In 1999, a political alliance between the Radical Party and a new political formation, FREPASO, won the general elections with promises to maintain the convertibility plan while fighting corruption, reducing unemployment and strengthening judicial independence. After less than a year in office, the government was accused of having bribed senators to approve a labour reform. The political alliance collapsed and the Radical Party was left to govern alone. President Fernando de la Rúa was incapable of rescuing the economy from the recession and, cornered by social demonstrations, resigned in December 2001 (Ollier 2001). In just a week, four presidents were appointed and quickly resigned. One of them, Adolfo Rodríguez Saá, declared a default on the national debt. Finally, Congress elected Eduardo Duhalde, who had been defeated in the 1999 general elections.

Although a weak president, Eduardo Duhalde managed to achieve economic and political stability. He called for national elections to be held in April 2013. Carlos Menem won 24 per cent of the national vote followed by Néstor Kirchner, who received 22 per cent. Both of them were Peronists but ran for the presidency with different political formations. As neither obtained a majority, a second round was needed, but Menem, fearing a defeat, stood down and Kirchner became president (Levitsky and Murillo 2008).

With only 22 per cent of the vote, Néstor Kirchner faced many challenges. After 2001, political parties were deeply fragmented. Indeed, the 2003 elections featured three different candidates from the Peronist Party and three from the Radical Party. Peronists failed to agree on a presidential candidate. Radicalism was divided, two candidates formed different parties, and one, Leopoldo Moreau, was the Radical candidate who received less than 3 per cent of the total vote. This fragmentation illustrated the delegitimization of politics that has been encapsulated by the slogan *que se vayan todos*.

With a weak mandate, Kirchner had to build political power in a volatile context. From the very beginning, he signalled change. First, he aimed to build power within Peronism, but also wanted to include left-wing political actors and parties. This was known as *transversalidad*, and its aim was to create a new political formation clearly identified with the left wing and what is known as *progresismo*. Kirchner was quite successful and a significant number of politicians and intellectuals joined his Frente para la Victoria. Secondly, Kirchner reformed the Supreme Court, which has been expanded by Carlos Menem from five to nine members. Menem created what was known as an 'automatic majority'; those new members approved most of the government's proposals. Kirchner pushed for the resignation of the new members, and in 2006 the Supreme Court reverted to its five-member status.[2] Thirdly, Kirchner reactivated a strong policy to prosecute those guilty of human rights violations during the 1976 military dictatorship. These three initiatives seemed to bring political renovation to the post-crisis scenario (Levitsky and Murillo 2008; Quiroga 2010).

However, President Kirchner very quickly did a U-turn, reverting to a traditional Peronist strategy of building up power and reducing judicial independence. Indeed, in 2005, when electoral lists needed to be organized, Kirchner turned to the General Confederation of Labour (CGT), which has been a traditional Peronist ally, and to the Peronist mayors of Buenos Aires Province. In order to build his power, Kirchner implemented a clientelist logic and made clear that, in Argentina, power is built through the executive (Quiroga 2010: 55).

Economic or political crises have been the excuse used by different democratic presidents to increase the power of the executive. Raúl Alfonsín, Carlos Menem, Fernando de la Rúa, Eduardo Duhalde, Néstor Kirchner and Cristina Fernández de Kirchner have adjusted the rule of law to their political purposes. This practice had been on the increase over the years, strengthening the power of the president and his/her autonomy. As a consequence, political institutions have become less important and more dependent on the executive's decisions. As Argentina has been in crisis mode pretty much continually since 1983, the concentration of power in the executive, as a requirement to resolve economic or political chaos, has become a key policy in this democratic era. Presidents increased their autonomy by taking power from the political parties and state institutions, especially the Congress. We would suggest that all the presidents since the return to democracy fall into two main categories: soft power usurper and ambivalent democrat (see Table 2.3 and 2.4).

While Raúl Alfonsín can be considered an ambivalent democrat, Carlos Menem, Fernando de la Rúa, Eduardo Duhalde, Néstor Kirchner and Cristina Fernández de Kirchner can be defined as soft power usurpers.

Raúl Alfonsín had the huge task of establishing democracy in Argentina. He could be considered as rule-obedient, receptive and a soft challenger. He promoted prosecution and punishment for those who committed human rights violations during the military dictatorship. However, after sentencing in the trial involving the *Juntas Militares*, Alfonsín tried to interfere in the justice system to avoid new trials against all military officers involved in human rights abuses. He also undermined the power of the Congress when, for instance, he changed the national currency by decree. However, he did respect civil rights and liberties and freedom of the press. He was tolerant but he did not try to achieve consensus with the Peronist Party or the trade unions; on the contrary, in his first months he promoted legislation which tried to neutralize the power of the unions. He did work with his cabinet and sporadically worked with some sectors of the Peronist opposition. He respected the power limits imposed by state institutions.

Carlos Menem, Fernando de la Rúa, Eduardo Duhalde, Néstor Kirchner and Cristina Fernández de Kirchner were closer to the definition of a soft power usurper. Most of them have been challenged by economic difficulties. These crises were not seen as a window of opportunity to reform politics or political parties; on the contrary, each crisis seemed to deepen undemocratic policies such as concentration of power in the executive, abuse of presidential decrees, interference in the justice system and use of clientelism to build political power and populism to secure power (see Table 2.4).

However, while Carlos Menem was quite successful in building and using autonomy from his political party and state institutions, Fernando de la Rúa and Eduardo Duhalde proved unable to build autonomy or concentrate power in their hands to maintain their position. An early conclusion is that a crisis or a post-crisis scenario per se does not guarantee that politicians can increase autonomy. A combination of domestic conditions and the leader's ability is more likely to explain the success of Menem, Néstor Kirchner and Cristina Fernández de Kirchner.

The reasons for the crisis in Ecuador

In Ecuador, economic instability and unpopular government decisions brought about the collapse of the political party system. Historically Ecuador had strong political leaders. Juan José Flores, José María Velasco Ibarra and León Febres Cordero are, among others, examples of the strong *caudillos* that have dominated Ecuador's political history. Political parties have also been historically significant. By the end of the 1990s, Ecuador's party system seemed to be consolidated around the Partido Social Cristiano, the Partido Roldosista Ecuatoriano, Izquierda Democrática and Democracia Popular. There were also new initiatives such as Movimiento Pachakutik.

Like other countries in the region, Ecuador was able to stabilize its economy at the beginning of the 1990s. Thanks to this stabilization, the country received foreign investment and achieved economic growth. However, in 1995, under the presidency of Sixto Durán Ballén, the war against Peru over a border dispute started a period of political and economic uncertainty that exploded in 2002.

In 1996 Abdalá Bucaram won the elections with the Partido Roldosista Ecuatoriano. As soon as he took office, he changed his economic preferences and turned from a populist strategy to a neoliberal one which promoted privatization and a currency scheme quite similar to the convertibility plan implemented in Argentina. While Carlos Menem in Argentina and Alberto Fujimori in Peru were able to transform themselves from populist to neoliberal advocates without jeopardizing their popularity, Bucaram could not. Seven months after he was elected, he faced a huge popular demonstration against the austerity measures and mounting corruption. Bucaram was impeached and political instability deepened. From his impeachment until Rafael Correa's election, Ecuador witnessed more economic instability and unpopular government decisions that finally caused the collapse of the political party system. There were seven presidents in less than ten years. After the 'dollarization' of the economy, President Jamil Mahuad was forced to resign in January 2000, leading to another period of political uncertainty that did not end when Lucio Gutiérrez won the 2002 general elections (Freidenberg 2008).

After participating in the 2000 coup against Mahuad, Gutiérrez formed the Partido Sociedad Patriótica, which, in an alliance with Movimiento Pachakutik, helped him to win the 2002 presidential elections (Van Cott 2008). Their platform was based on the transformation of the neoliberal agenda and the fight against corruption; but, once he was in office, Gutiérrez reversed his strategy and was unable to maintain his power. He broke his political alliance with left-wing parties and moved closer to the conservative Partido Social Cristiano (PSC). However, this alliance did not last very long and the PSC and Movimiento Pachakutik pushed for Gutiérrez's impeachment (Montúfar 2008). He was finally dismissed in 2005 owing to increasing social unrest and demonstrations, which were held mainly in Quito. As in Argentina, the slogan was *que se vayan todos*. But in Ecuador this became a reality. The political party system collapsed and a thoroughgoing revival of the political elite took place. The traditional parties, from both left and right, were discredited. Former finance minister Rafael Correa won the 2006 presidential elections and assumed office in January 2007. He presented a strong discourse against the so-called *partidocracia* ('partycracy', a negative term used to describe old, traditional political parties). He did not present candidates for the legislative branch, paving the way for its transformation. The new assembly was formed in 2008, with a somewhat renewed political elite.

Lucio Gutiérrez and Rafael Correa had some similarities. They could be considered outsiders and newcomers and both were highly critical of the political system, promoting an *antisistema* discourse. So what are the reasons that explain Gutiérrez's failure and Correa's success? Martín Tanaka (2013) argues that Rafael Correa benefited from oil price increases. Thus, Tanaka answers the question combining leadership and economic conditions. During 2005, revenues from oil increased by 40 per cent (El Universo 2005). Ecuador enjoyed record-breaking oil prices from 2007 to 2012 (El Comercio 2013). Not surprisingly, Correa's government has taken advantage of this situation. However, the oil boom in itself cannot be considered the only reason behind Correa's success. His ability to capitalize on the oil price increase also needs to be taken into consideration.

Rafael Correa became minister of finance when Alfredo Palacio succeeded Lucio Gutiérrez. In his four months as minister, he achieved high popularity. He promoted a closer relationship with Venezuela while being critical of the pressures from the World Bank to implement austerity measures and the negotiations for a free trade agreement with the United States. Like Hugo Chávez in Venezuela, Correa understood the dissatisfaction of citizens with the neoliberal agenda, the role of the multinational institutions and the austerity measures. He built up his political discourse, emphasizing Ecuador's sovereignty. Finally, seven months after leaving the government, Correa founded a political movement, Patria Altiva i Soberana (Proud and Sovereign Fatherland), whose objectives were political sovereignty, regional integration and poverty relief. Correa understood the political mood that dominated Ecuador at that time.

The political turmoil that Ecuador was witnessing had some similarities with the background to the emergence of Hugo Chávez in Venezuela and Evo Morales in Bolivia. In the case of Ecuador, traditional parties and new actors such as Partido Sociedad Patriótica or Movimiento Pachakutik proved unable to tackle the economic and political crisis that affected the country from 1995. This caused the relationship between the citizens and their representatives to break down. Gutiérrez's electoral win showed that citizens were ready to accept outsiders with the mandate to transform the system. While Gutiérrez did not particularly promote change in the economy, Rafael Correa proposed a complete political and economic renovation (Mainwaring 2008).

First, Correa represented a unifying figure in a historically divided country: between the coast and the Andes, between the urban and rural environments and many ethnic divisions. He is one of few political leaders who has been able to develop a national leadership. Secondly, Correa has transformed clientelism by centralizing and institutionalizing it through the plan *Bono de Desarrollo Humano*. According to data from the Ministry of Social and Economic Inclusion (MIES), in 2014 approximately 1.9 million people qualified to receive the *Bono* – a monthly benefit of US$50, for families living below the poverty line, as defined by the Ministry of Social Development. Traditionally, clientelism in Ecuador was mainly conducted at the local level as a negotiation tool between local barons and urban elites, particularly in Quito and Guayaquil. Political parties were territorially based and structured more locally than ideologically. Gradually, these became more involved in representing local interests and closely related to local clientelist networks. Rafael Correa severed these ties and managed to impose direct clientelism without intermediaries, ignoring local barons. The *Bono de Desarrollo Humano* is nationally distributed through an electronic card and cashpoints; so no local intermediaries are required. Thirdly, Correa's attacks on political parties turned out to be very popular. He rejected political parties from the very beginning, and this strategy has been so successful that politicians are still cautious about mentioning the rebirth of political parties (Conaghan and De la Torre 2008; De la

Torre 2013a). The collapse of the political party system prompted a high degree of turnover, with the inclusion of young people and women following that of indigenous movements.

In a context of low institutionalization Correa appeared able to take the country out of a period of political stagnation. He was perceived by many as the solution to Ecuador's deep economic and political crisis. However, he gradually became a polarizing leader, with a tendency to concentrate power and use populist and clientelist tactics (De la Torre 2013b). Like many leaders before him, he attempted to consolidate power by presenting himself as the only solution and the only representative of the people. Moreover, the 2013 elections show that the political system has not recovered. Rafael Correa won with 57 per cent of the total vote followed by Guillermo Lasso, a businessman who created a political formation to present its candidacy. Lasso received 22 per cent of the total vote followed by Lucio Gutiérrez with only 6 per cent. Politics in Ecuador is divided between an opposition still open to newcomers and outsiders and a concentration of power in Correa's hands.

As in the Argentine case, it seems that in Ecuador leaders make a difference. Rafael Correa achieved what Abdalá Bucaram, Lucio Gutiérrez and others could not accomplish. Before Rafael Correa came on the scene, Ecuador had seven presidents in ten years. The list starts in 1997 with the fall of Abdalá Bucaram. Five presidents occupied the Palacio de Carondelet (Fabián Alarcón, Jamil Mahuad, Gustavo Noboa, Lucio Gutiérrez and Alfredo Palacio) until political stability was achieved with the arrival of Rafael Correa. In this context, it is difficult to categorize them within our typology of leaders because they stayed in government for short periods of time. They were unable to develop any leadership style either because they were inefficient – probably they did not have the ability to lead – or because they were thrown out by social mobilizations owing to their incapacity to stabilize the economy or to avoid adjustment policies.

Leaders such as Carlos Menem, Néstor Kirchner and Rafael Correa had the ability to interpret people's needs and expectations, to communicate charismatically their objectives, to gain people's trust and to build political power. Our typology can be applied to those who have the ability to lead. In Ecuador, after many years of political chaos, Rafael Correa was able to take the country out of its misery.

The post-crisis scenarios

In Argentina, the 2001 post-crisis scenario brought to the fore the existing fragmentation of traditional political parties, but also a significant degree of turnover at the municipal level and in the national Congress. After the crisis, new political parties emerged: Coalición Cívica in 2002; Propuesta Republicana in 2005; and Generación para un Nuevo Encuentro Nacional in 2007. However, only 12 per cent of respondents in Argentina believed that new actors had been incorporated in the post-crisis political system and only 28 per cent thought that political practices had actually changed.

The country seems to have moved from its traditional two-party system to one with a (fragmented) dominant party surrounded by new small parties or Peronist splits. The Peronist Party is not only fragmented and contradictory, but is also highly decentralized, with different leaders fighting to control as many political barons as possible in an attempt to conquer national power. This scenario is not very different from the preceding one: one leader monopolizes power at the top while many politicians fight against each other to praise 'the one and only' so as eventually to succeed him.

In this regard, the diagnosis was conclusive: 74 per cent of the legislators interviewed opined that the main political problem in Argentina is the combination of strong leaders with weak political parties. The main political parties have been unable to change the historic trend of strong leaders. The Radical Party has been dominated by Hipólito Yrigoyen, Leandro Alem, Ricardo Balbín and Raúl Alfonsín, and Peronism by Juan Perón, Carlos Menem and Néstor and Cristina Kirchner. Political parties in Argentina seem to need strong leaders to win elections and maintain power. In this context, political parties can become flexible, functional institutions at the service of the leader.

On the other hand, around 30 per cent of legislators believed that parties are also chameleons, deserting and dumping leaders when these become powerless. Thus, parties in Argentina seem to be considered as power machines that only serve strong leaders. Fifty-seven per cent of respondents also argued that most political parties lack ideas, can switch ideologies readily and opportunistically, and that leaders are prepared to break from their parties to increase personal power. Party discipline is absent and leaders easily jump from one party to another. Although most interviewees argued that the main feature of Argentina's political system is the lack of rules, we did find a set of clear and concise 'rules' that are used to increase and maintain power. Politics is a process of power construction through a clientelist logic of exchanging votes, jobs or money. In Argentina, power is achieved through different clientelist channels. Provincial political barons in government are able to distribute a high number of public posts and manage public funds that are crucial to maintaining their clientelist networks. Thanks to this political and economic power, provincial barons usually hold the key to presenting names for the electoral lists. Once elected, these political leaders continue to exchange votes for money, loyalty, support or jobs. These exchanges occur among legislators, politicians in the executive, local political barons and clients. The exchange is political capital, which helps politicians maintain their power, job and privileges. The national leader builds his power by keeping wide networks of clientelist relations, exchanging national funds for the control of provinces, political support for re-elections, jobs and social programmes

(Lodola 2009; Szwarcberg 2012). As a result of this individually driven power-building process, political parties remain on the margins.

Clientelism is a tool used by a power usurper to increase his power. In the Argentine case, we observed that politicians – national leaders or provincial barons – practise clientelism as power usurpers. These clientelist networks were widely explained in the interviews. When asked whether these are the complex steps of political negotiations, 88 per cent of interviewees considered that, rather than building consensus or aiming to agree on political issues, the main goal of these processes was to maintain individual power, benefits and privileges. In fact, clientelism was considered a permanent feature: 84 per cent of our respondents argued that clientelism, conceptualized as a tool to increase power through the use and abuse of public resources, was impossible to eradicate. Moreover, 65 per cent answered that clientelism persisted because it was essential to the type of political domination exercised by politicians. Thus, it can be concluded that politics does have clear 'rules' and that leaders can build up personal power independent of political parties. From the long conversations held with politicians, the puzzle of the Argentine case is expressed in the relationship between a low degree of institutionalization of political parties and the autonomy of strong political leaders.

In Ecuador, Correa and his new PAIS movement were seen by 45 per cent of our respondents (including some from the opposition) as a fresh start in a politically stagnant country. However, the renewal of the political elite did not break with old political practices: 90 per cent of our respondents argued that clientelism continues to be a strong political tool. Moreover, Ecuador has always had strong political leaders. Rafael Correa continues that tradition. However, some changes were identified.

A considerable number of respondents, 48 per cent, agreed that during the Correa administration there have been innovations in political practices: 42 per cent of them referred to innovations in communication methods between politicians and citizens; 41 per cent referred to innovations being due to the inclusion of new actors and 17 per cent saw innovations in the degree of the government's transparency.

The collapse of the political party system prompted a high degree of turnover, with the inclusion of young people and women following that of indigenous movements. Studies on elite circulation are rare in Ecuador. Some of the available bibliography centres on the study of the candidates for the 2007 Constitutional Assembly. Of the candidates interviewed for that study, 75.5 per cent had not held political office before and 79.6 per cent had not previously held a job in a political party. Only 34.7 per cent had begun their political career in a political party (Freidenberg 2008). Despite these newcomers, the Assembly followed historical trends: 50 per cent of its members had university degrees, 38.8 per cent had postgraduate degrees and 43.7 per cent had undertaken postgraduate studies abroad. In a country where only 11 per cent of the population goes to university (Viteri Díaz 2006), despite Correa's Citizen Revolution, the assembly was co-opted by a small elite. In 2010, according to data from the Legislative Assembly's website, 82.2 per cent of its members had a university degree.

Thus, the changes that Correa achieved are combined with a significant degree of continuity. Rafael Correa was perceived by many as the solution to Ecuador's deep economic and political crisis; however, he gradually became a polarizing leader, with a tendency to concentrate power and use populist and clientelist tactics (De la Torre 2013b). Like many leaders before him, he attempted to consolidate power in a personalized fashion, presenting himself as the only solution and the only representative of the people.

As in Argentina, in Ecuador clientelism is considered a structural problem and a tool for political domination: in Quito 56 per cent of our respondents defined clientelism as the use and abuse of public resources to gain political benefits. On the other hand, 34 per cent emphasized that citizens exhibited a clientelist logic: they expected some type of benefit in exchange for their participation in politics. Clientelism is a two-way problem, where responsibility falls on politicians as well as citizens. While Correa neutralized the power of local barons, 90 per cent of our respondents agreed that clientelism is still used as a tool to maintain power through a network of exchanges of benefits for political loyalty.

We have identified different types of clientelism and divided them into horizontal and vertical clientelism. Horizontal clientelism is the exchange of political favours and/or money for political support among politicians, i.e. between legislators in the National Congress, between legislators and provincial barons or members of the executive. Vertical clientelism is that between politicians and political supporters. While politics in Argentina seems to have both types, Ecuador is more prone to the vertical model. While in Argentina 47 per cent of respondents mentioned horizontal clientelism, in Ecuador only 10 per cent referred to it. In Ecuador, 56 per cent considered clientelism as a misuse of public resources to obtain political benefits and 34 per cent recognized it as a tool to exchange votes for benefits. Therefore, 90 per cent of our Ecuadorean respondents recognized the existence of what we considered vertical clientelism.

In Argentina, horizontal clientelism was described by 47 per cent of our respondents. They used catchphrases such as *dos contratos por una ley* (referring to the exchange of jobs in Congress for positive support for legislation) or *política del trueque* (barter politics). In Ecuador, vertical clientelism was summarized as *quien más da, más votos recibe* (meaning the politician that gives the most gets the majority of votes).

Clientelism, personalism and weak or fragmented political parties were the main features of the post-crisis scenario identified by most of our respondents in both Argentina and Ecuador. There are some significant differences. In Argentina, traditional political parties, such as the Peronists and Radicals, were weakened by the crisis and became very fragmented. New parties emerged and there was a slow but constant turnover of elites. In Ecuador, most of the traditional parties lost power and representation; they are struggling to survive or re-emerge in a context of a thoroughgoing and fast elite revival. However, both political systems are still embedded in old political practices: clientelism as a political tool that opens up doors for political corruption and excessive presidentialism or personalism with strong leaders who embrace populism as a tool to decrease the number of veto players, weakening the system of checks and balances and the level of political accountability.

The responses of our interviewees helped us to design our classification of leaders. Argentina and Ecuador offer key guidelines for exploring the main features of soft power usurpers. In both cases, the economic chaos was an excuse to usurp power from other state institutions and increase the power of the president.

Conceptualizing political leadership

Argentina

In Argentina our respondents characterized leaders as strong or weak according to their ability to accumulate power. The interviews gave a clear message: 64 per cent of our interviewees believed that political leadership was decadent. The story told by our respondents showed strong leaders, a low degree of institutionalization of political parties, low party competition and unstable and flexible rules. Most of the leaders in Argentina seem to encapsulate the features of rule challenger, soft polarizer and power builder. The interviews in Argentina were conducted during the first presidency of Cristina Fernández de Kirchner and thus we mainly discussed her leadership style.

Cristina Fernández de Kirchner was first elected to the Santa Cruz legislature in 1991. Between 1995 and 2007, she was repeatedly elected to the National Congress, both as deputy and senator. When her husband, President Néstor Kirchner, announced that he would not seek re-election in 2007, Cristina was promoted as his successor. She won the 2007 elections with almost 45 per cent of the total vote. She was the candidate of the Frente Para la Victoria (Front for Victory), a political organization which included mainly Peronists, members of the Radical Party and of small parties from the left. Her vice-president was Julio Cobos from the Radical Party.

Between rule challenger and rule-obedient

Fernández de Kirchner is a leader who combines elements of soft power usurper and ambivalent democrat. Respondents mentioned the use of clientelism and populism to increase her personal power, the concentration of power in the executive to legislate in key areas, together with respect for democratic rights, civil liberties and freedom of press. She can be considered a rule challenger and rule-obedient. Indeed, when her attempts to modify or implement new rules were not successful, she accepted these results. This was the case with Resolution 125 which pitted the government against the agricultural sector.

Cristina Fernández had, at the very beginning of her government, an absolute majority in Congress. Taking advantage of this majority she promoted an increase in the agricultural export tax. This would be the third increase in one year. Resolution 125 indicated that the tax would be flexible, which meant that it would increase or decrease following price fluctuations. The increase that the president was proposing in March 2008 was from 35 per cent to 44 per cent for soya beans and from 32 per cent to 39 per cent for sunflower seeds. This proposal prompted a major confrontation with the agricultural exporters. Historically, Argentina's economy has been agriculture-led. Moreover, landowners and agricultural export-ers, from big or small farms, had been historically anti-Peronist. However, Fernández de Kirchner had won in many small towns in rural areas so she seemed to have the support of the owners of small farms. Despite this, there was strong opposition to the new increase. This was a turning point for her government and her first big political failure. The resolution was not approved in the Congress. The negative vote of her vice-president, the Radical Julio Cobos, buried the government's proposal. She did, however, accept the result.

There was another political confrontation in which Fernández de Kirchner was able to accept her limits. The executive power in Argentina has the capacity to legislate through the Necessity and Urgency Decrees (NUDs). They are issued by the president and have the force of law. According to the 1994 Constitution they can be used in exceptional circumstances.[3] The president has used NUDs to introduce changes in the national budget, to approve the use of national reserves to pay the debt, to implement social programmes, to nationalize the pension funds and to regulate private provision of health services. The use of national reserves to pay the debt was reduced by the president of the Central Bank, who was later sacked, and by the justice system. Finally, the president had to annul the first NUD and issue a new one (Levy Yeyati and Novaro 2013). In this case, Fernández made some concessions but got her way and the government was able to use the Central Bank reserves to pay the debt. She explained her tactics by saying 'if we go backwards, we do it to gain strength and jump further' (ibid.: 218).

Our respondents agreed that leaders in Argentina have to be strong. Sixty-two per cent argued that strong leaders are a necessity because there are no rules and the political parties are weak. One senator emphasized that 'Argentines like authoritarian leaders, those who are above the law. These leaders give us security and stability.

We do not realize that those leaders will end up abusing power. They will become a problem. In every crisis we look for someone who is going to rescue us.' Cristina Fernández was considered one of those strong leaders. Rather than rescuing Argentina from a crisis, her role was to continue what her husband had started. Both aimed to rebuild the state, which had collapsed in 2001, to change the economic strategy, emphasizing the role of the government in the management of the economy, and to rewrite national history. They were able to pursue their objectives thanks to the soya boom which helped Argentina's economy to recover with 9 per cent economic growth in 2010 and 2011.

While the majority of our respondents seemed to prefer strong leaders, 46 per cent argued that collective leadership should be promoted, pointing to the examples of the Frente Amplio in Uruguay and the Concertación in Chile. However, 73 per cent of interviewees pointed out that a sizeable majority of Argentines understand political leadership as individual and authoritarian. This perspective is confirmed by politics in Argentina. As one deputy said, 'the history of political parties is monopolized by the history of their leaders'. Forty-four per cent stated that this type of leader does not promote political renovation. For instance, 32 per cent of respondents from the Radical Party pointed out that Raúl Alfonsín became, in the long term, one of the most important obstacles to the renovation of the Radical Party. One member of his government argued that Alfonsín concentrated power in his hands, blocking the inclusion of new, younger members.

Thus, Fernández de Kirchner was no exception – a strong, powerful leader who challenged the rules while at the same time accepting some of the limits imposed by the law and state institutions. As one political leader told us, 'leaders in Argentina are always trying to challenge the law and the institutions. If they succeed, they go ahead. If they fail, they will accept the limits and try again later or by other means.'

Not so soft a polarizer

The Argentine president is closer to a power usurper. She is a polar-izer, intolerant, and does not share power in the decision-making process. She concentrates power in her hands and takes decisions with a small circle of advisers; some of them are not part of her cabinet.

The polarization of Argentine society was exacerbated under her leadership, most specifically during the 2008 confronta-tion with the agricultural sector. The old Peronist confrontation between the working class and the oligarchy came alive. Although she lost her battle there, it was a historical moment with two main legacies.

First, a new Peronist movement emerged. La Cámpora[4] is a youth organization that was formed by Máximo Kirchner, son of Cristina and Néstor. It firmly supports the Kirchner government. Many of its members are the children of Peronist militants of the 1970s who dis-appeared during the military dictatorship. Fernández de Kirchner appointed a significant number of its members to her adminis-tration. Secondly, Fernández de Kirchner's image was damaged because of her failure to pass Resolution 125, and she lost the legis-lative elections in 2009. So the legacy of the confrontation with the agricultural sector was mixed. On the one hand, while La Cámpora was created in 2003, it was after the confrontation that it emerged nationally as a strong, very active, supporter of the government. On the other hand, the government was weakened by losing its majority in Congress.

The emergence of a new movement renewed the government. Paradoxically, the renovation meant the resurrection of old Peronist styles, and Fernández de Kirchner deepened the polarization of society between her followers and her detractors. Her government became involved in a long confrontation with a media conglomer-ate, Grupo Clarín. This fight also started during the confrontation with the agricultural sector. The Grupo Clarín owned one of the main newspapers as well as TV channels and many radio stations. The government proposed a law to limit the power of the conglomerate. The law, known as *Ley de Medios* (Media Law), established certain rules and procedures for the distribution of TV and radio licences. It was passed in 2009. Grupo Clarín appealed but its appeal was rejected by the Supreme Court in 2013. This means that all media conglomerates have to adjust their size according to the new law. The battle was won by the government. In the meantime, the confrontation exacerbated the political polarization. Our respondents portrayed a scenario which was highly divided between those who followed Cristina Fernández and those who opposed her. One senator pointed out that the government was damaging the democratic system through the promotion of political confrontation. Sixty-three per cent of interviewees argued that the president attempted to increase her power by undermining political actors. One deputy who belonged to the Peronist Party had a different opinion: 'the president is strengthening democracy by limiting the power of powerful newspapers'.

Power builder and maximizer

Both Kirchners were described in our interviews as power builders and power maximizers. Clientelism, as a tool to use and abuse state revenues, and concentration of power were the main pillars that took Néstor Kirchner from his weak beginning to becoming another strongman in Argentina's politics. There are two legal tools behind these pillars: the co-participation law (23.548), which was passed in 1988 as a transitory regime, is still in place, and the emergency law (25.561), passed during the 2002 crisis, has been extended until December 2015. These two laws, together with decrees from the executive, allow the government to use resources from outside the national budget. Some economists have argued that since

2003 the government was able to access, without the approval of parliament, around US$52 million that can be used discretionally (Clarín 2011). By undermining the inflation rate and economic growth figures, the government has been able to receive more revenues than those included in the national budget. Thanks to the NUD issued by the executive and the discretion allowed by the emergency co-participation laws, both the Kirchner administrations have been able to use state resources to build political power.

Ideologically they were both very strong and articulated. They promoted a different narrative (*el relato*) which attempted to create a hegemonic discourse. In 2003, the Congress annulled the Full Stop and the Due Obedience laws which were passed during the Alfonsín government to limit the number of trials against those who committed human rights violations. In 2004, in the Military Academy, Kirchner ordered that the portraits of General Jorge Rafael Videla and Reynaldo Bignone, who were de facto presidents during the dictatorship, be taken down. These were symbolic gestures to show that the government was committed to the defence of human rights. Both Néstor and Cristina Kirchner structured a discourse which argued that nothing had been done to tackle historical human rights violations under successive democratic governments.

There was further manipulation of information with the intervention of the National Institute of Statistics and Census (INDEC) in January 2007. The idea behind the intervention was to control data, especially when the inflation rate began to escalate (Levy Yeyati and Novaro 2013).

In our interviews, both Néstor Kirchner and Cristina Fernández de Kirchner were portrayed as leaders who would use any tool to maximize power. The laws, the new narrative and the intervention of the INDEC are examples of tools that challenge the rule of law. They both defied the institutions of the state and attempted to ignore rules. Ideologically they have been strong and highly articulated, which has helped to undermine an already weak political opposition.

Ecuador

Political leaders have had a profound effect on Ecuador. Many of those we interviewed agreed that Ecuadorean history can be told by talking about its leaders, including the incumbent president, Rafael Correa.[5] Eighty-six per cent of our interviewees defined Ecuadorean political leaders as strong and keen to monopolize power. Analysis of Correa's leadership pointed to polarization and a permanent debate that we heard in all the interviews. Correa engenders strong confrontational feelings and opinions. According to our respondents, Correa combines elements of a power usurper and a soft power usurper. At the very beginning of his presidency, he could be considered a democratic enhancer, since he promoted the building of democratic institutions such as the 2008 Constitution and the new Assembly.

Rule challenger and rule developer

From the very beginning, Rafael Correa challenged state institutions. He wanted to re-create the state, limit the power of old political actors and traditional political parties, transform the economy, leaving behind the neoliberal strategy, increase social expenditure and achieve sovereignty in the energy and the financial sector. For the 2007 elections he did not have candidates for the Congress. One of our respondents pointed out that Correa considered the Congress and the traditional political parties 'responsible for Ecuador's political decadence'. As soon as he took office, he asked the Tribunal Supremo Electoral (Supreme Electoral Tribunal) to organize a referendum to ask citizens about the formation of a Constituent Assembly. The Tribunal sent his proposal to Congress, where Correa had only marginal support. Fifty-seven congressmen opposed the initiative. The Tribunal dismissed them because they were blocking an electoral process. Correa supported that decision. This was the first confrontation that Correa had with a state institution. One of the dismissed congressmen told us that 'it became clear that Correa was breaking down the traditional political regime'. Indeed, in order to re-create the state, Correa had to dissolve the old regime. In this period, he presented elements of a power usurper and a democratic enhancer since he undermined and rebuilt democratic institutions.

His proposal to form a Constituent Assembly succeeded with 81 per cent of the total vote. In the elections to form the Assembly, Correa's movement Alianza PAIS won almost 70 per cent of the total vote. The Constituent Assembly wrote a new Constitution, which was ratified by a referendum with 63.9 per cent of the vote. With significant popular support, Correa had changed the main pillars of the state.

Gradually, Correa started a confrontation with the press through the judiciary. In 2011, he began a judicial process against the newspaper *El Universal*. The paper had strongly criticized Correa's management of the police revolt of 2010. The newspaper called the president a dictator who had committed crimes against humanity by ordering people to fire at the policemen. The trial ended with a victory for Correa. *El Universal* had to pay 40 million dollars in compensation and the director and some journalists were sentenced to three years in jail. Finally, Correa pardoned them. Before and after this case, the relationship between the president and the opposition media had been tense. The interviews reflected this polarization. Respondents who supported the president blamed the media for trying to demonize Correa. Other interviewees argued that the president had undermined press freedom because he could not accept any criticism. It is interesting to highlight that 37 per cent of our respondents who supported the president agreed that Correa did not accept 'no for an answer and found it very difficult to accept any criticism'.

In 2011, the president promoted a referendum to modify some articles from the 2008 Constitution and from the Penal Code. Issues related to public security, environment, justice, the banking system and the media were affected. There were ten questions, some of them quite complex. The results were tight. In some of the questions the sum of the negative answers, the blank answers and the invalid ones was higher than that for the affirmative answer. However, Correa said that only the valid votes should be considered, which meant his proposal succeeded.

These examples show that Rafael Correa began as a democratic enhancer promoting a new Constitution which could be considered as one of the most progressive in the region.[6] He was gradually becoming a soft power usurper by confronting the press, polarizing society and increasing his personal power. According to 55 per cent of the interviewees, Correa believes that the whole process of transformation came from him. This means that President Rafael Correa does not consider his leadership to be a relationship with his supporters in a specific time and space but rather a range of personal qualities which has led him to become the unopposed leader of Ecuador since 2007. Several opinions voiced in the interviews suggest that the president considers himself to be the only representative of the will of the people (whether supporter or opponent, citizen or politician) so the only options for everyone else are to stand with him or alone.

Our interviewees highlighted one quality about the president in particular – that he believes in generational change so that the government includes plenty of young bureaucrats. A former adviser to the president said that on coming to power 'they clashed with the existing institutions and the 1998 Constitution' but over time the drive to innovate weakened and all that was left was a desire to remain in office, thanks in particular to the popularity of the president.

Thus far Correa has achieved and appears able to maintain leadership for the nation as a whole. This is considered by many interviewees as a very important political achievement, since Ecuador is in many respects a divided country – divided between mountains and coast, urban and rural areas. Another of the president's achievements, according to the interviewees, is the government's social conscience, which is a marked change from the past.

Correa has transformed clientelism by centralizing and institutionalizing it by means of the *Bono de Desarrollo Humano* (Human Development Bonus) plan. However, while this has provided much-needed social investment, it has also been plagued with inefficiency and corruption and limited citizen participation. A so-called 'bonocracy'[7] has also sprung up. This refers to the exchange of *Bonos* for support for the government. Thirty-six per cent of our interviewees agreed that institutionalized clientelism was very obvious in this government and that populist approaches and traditional strongman leaders persist.

A complex combination of democratic enhancer and soft power usurper, President Rafael Correa was the main topic of conversation in all the interviews. While our respondents agreed that he is a national leader who has been able to transform Ecuador, those in opposition fear that he is forgetting his democratic values and beginning to approximate our power usurper model. For instance, 47 per cent of our interviewees expressed doubts about the relationship between the government and the Constitution. They maintained that the Constitution could end up being a 'straitjacket' if the government continues to increase its personalist and authoritarian characteristics. One PAIS legislator pointed to the obvious contradiction between an almost perfect Constitution and the government. He said 'PAIS should demand that the President adhere more closely to the Constitution'.

Polarizer

Rafael Correa considers his leadership to be pivotal in helping Ecuador to begin a new process of independence (De la Torre 2013a). His discourse has polarized society by accusing traditional political parties of being responsible for the many crises that the country has faced since the 1990s. The president perceives himself as the only force behind the Citizens' Revolution (*Revolución Ciudadana*). Those who opposed his plans have been labelled traitors. He has confronted all of them: the *partidocracia*, the press (criticized as mediocre and corrupt by the president) and the old style left, especially indigenous movements and ecologists (ibid.).

The interviews in Quito gave us a strong feeling of the polarization and intolerance that abound in politics. We were able to interview five politicians (members of the Assembly and former members of Correa's government) who had become deeply disillusioned. They argued that Correa had 'kidnapped the spirit of the 2008 Constitution' and his main objective was to maintain his power. The innovative and revolutionary feeling of the first years was gone. The government was described as a 'technocratic government that discouraged social movements and debate'. They portrayed Correa as intolerant and obsessed with personal power. One of our respondents argued that Correa has developed a messianic discourse: 'he is the people'. He told us that many times the president used phrases such as 'I am the leader, I am the one who got the votes, I know what has to be done'.

One of the interviewees referred to Correa as an icon who combines the beginning and the end, who can promote passion and become the centre of the universe, the one who decides who is bad and who is good: 'every Saturday he stops at the pulpit and reads the gospel for that week'.[8] There is no doubt that Correa arouses strong conflicting feeling and opinions. A close collaborator of the government who left described Correa as a very intelligent academic, a clever man with a great capacity for leadership but with little political experience and somebody who 'cannot understand and never has understood that he is only in power because society as a whole generated the right conditions'. According to one of the young leaders, who founded Ruptura de los 25, his experience of the political ascent of Correa is that: 'in Ecuador building up leadership requires you to show strength'.

Power maximizer

Many of our respondents began to admire Rafael Correa in 2005 when he was finance minister. It was clear then that he had the ability to lead. His discourse concentrated on recovering Ecuador's sovereignty. This helped him to become very popular. Among our respondents, 56 per cent believed that Correa was 'the solution for the country'. However, 34 per cent of them stated that the president has also become a problem.

One of the main problems mentioned was the lack of political parties. However, 87 per cent of the interviewees firmly rejected them. One of them even said, 'political parties do not exist any more'. A government minister was one of the few people who suggested that the political parties were something that still needed to be sorted out and that the traditional parties needed to be restructured to take into account the changes in Ecuadorean society since 2007.

One of the politicians we interviewed summed up recent party history: 'When the democratic process began in 1979 there were three types of party: the old traditional parties that had existed for many years, such as the conservatives and socialists, the new ideological parties (Democratic Left and Popular Left) and the new populist parties (Concentration of Popular Forces). Under democratic rule the parties began to adopt populist practices while the old parties disappeared. The new parties also adopted clientelist practices with strong leaderships, corporativism and short-term policy vision'. According to our respondents, before 2007 there were three main political actors: strong leaders, weak political parties and citizens who took to the streets each time they were politically dissatisfied.

Opposition leaders agreed that the political party system in Ecuador had failed, but they mainly blamed Correa for the dismantling of the parties. Seventy-nine per cent of the opposition politicians we interviewed agreed that government assaults on the political parties had been very effective, so much so that many party leaders were ashamed of their parties. Indeed, Correa's attacks on political parties turned out to be very popular. He rejected political parties from the very beginning, and this strategy has been so successful that politicians are still cautious about mentioning the rebirth of political parties. One leader maintained that the president had demonized politics and politicians and that nowadays many leaders say repeatedly 'I am not a politician'. Political parties' reputations are so damaged that most interviewees prefer to regard their organizations as 'movements'. It is definitely the case that the decline of the political parties was also directly related to their lack of transparency, their understanding of politics as merely a means of peddling influence and privileges for one sector of society. It was also related to the lack of institutionalization, which also affects the state as a whole.

Conclusion

The scenarios that arise out of crises show similarities and differences. In the two countries new leaders came to power. While Néstor Kirchner and Cristina Fernández de Kirchner were traditional but marginal politicians, Rafael Correa was an *outsider*. The three were launched on to the national scene because of a power vacuum following the crisis. The severity of the crisis was used as an excuse to justify the usurpation of power. The concentration of power in the executive was absorbed into an image of democratic stability and governability.

Argentina and Ecuador show that a post-crisis scenario increases the likelihood that soft power usurpers or power usurpers will emerge. The analysis of the four countries presented so far shows the need to contextualize the study of leaders. Leaders are not born in isolation; they are the product of political parties and the political careers that they develop within the party's rules. If parties are in decline, fragmented, clientelist and dysfunctional; if rules are flexible and uncertain and if discipline is absent, and accountability and transparency are low or non-existent, then the likelihood of having usurpers increases. The winner-takes-all logic, together with a lack of pluralism, tolerance and consensus politics, also explains the emergence of usurpers.

In the case of Argentina and Ecuador it was important to recall the bibliography on the halo effect to tackle the degree of polarization among our respondents: some demonize the Kirchners and Correa, others love them. This was also essential to analyse our following case, Venezuela. This country experienced a collapse of its party system and the emergence of a unique leader, Hugo Chávez. We now apply our typology to the case of the charismatic leader who radically transformed Venezuela.

CHAPTER 5

Leadership in the Context of the Collapse of a Party System: Venezuela

Introduction

Venezuela combines strong political parties and strong leaders such as Rómulo Betancourt, Carlos Andrés Pérez and the dictator Marcos Pérez Jimenez. These leaders were strong *caudillos* with a populist approach. They appealed to nationalistic sentiment with a clever use of political symbols. Political parties were also strong. Acción Democrática was founded in 1941 and COPEI (Comité de Organización Política Electoral Independiente) in 1946. Both parties dominated Venezuelan politics from the 1940s to the 1990s. The end of the so-called *democracia pactada* (Karl 1986; Magdaleno 2013) meant the collapse of the traditional political parties and the emergence of a new strong leader.

In this chapter, we present an analysis of fifty-seven interviews conducted in Caracas between October 2011 and March 2012. This is a very different chapter from the others. On one hand, we were unable to interview any member of the Partido Socialista Unido de Venezuela (PSUV, United Socialist Party of Venezuela), any member of the government or any journalist who supported Hugo

Chávez. All our efforts to persuade them of the academic nature of our research were in vain. According to the opposition leaders the negative answers could be because members of the PSUV and the government did not want to be seen with foreigners and were suspicious about how their words would be used. Nobody wanted to take the risk of being quoted in a foreign newspaper. The PSUV, it was explained to us, is a very hierarchical organization and its members would not risk their position by meeting with us. Therefore we interviewed only members of the opposition parties such as Movement for Socialism (Movimiento al Socialismo), Radical Cause (Causa Radical), the Red Flag Party (Partido Bandera Roja), Project Venezuela (Proyecto Venezuela), A New Era (Un Nuevo Tiempo), Justice First (Primero Justicia) and For Social Democracy (Por la Democracia Social, PODEMOS) and other parties from the Mesa de Unidad Democrática (MUD).

On the other hand, when we arrived in Caracas in October 2011, the nation was still in shock after the announcement in June that the president had cancer. Moreover, the political opposition was reorganizing itself to present candidates for the primary elections in February 2012. For the first time they would present a candidate for the presidential elections who would be elected in open primaries. The illness of the president and the primaries were the main worries of our interviewees. We had to make enormous efforts to keep the interviews focused on our questionnaire. We have to confess that often the interviews took a long time because it was fascinating to listen to all the rumours about Chávez's health and to all the analysis of the primaries' results.

In order to comply with the structure of the book, we have decided not to include the multiple political scenarios that were presented to us in the interviews. In this chapter, as in the previous chapters, we are analysing the post-crisis scenario, the emergence of Hugo Chávez and the conceptualization of political leaders as presented in the interviews.

The reasons for the crisis

Although it came as a surprise, the ease with which the Venezuelan political party system was dismantled could have been foreseen if historical details had been deeply analysed. After the 1958 political agreement, the political party system became highly institutionalized with a very low degree of electoral competition. The options were scarce: the Christian Democratic Party, known as COPEI, and Democratic Action (AD), which was the social democratic option.

The *Punto Fijo* accord consolidated a democratic regime with two well-established political parties and a low degree of electoral competition. The aim of the pact was to achieve political stability and to avoid the return of authoritarian regimes. The 1958 pact implemented a shared government since the parties committed themselves to accept election results and to include members of AD and COPEI in each government. Although this was seen as one of the pillars of Venezuelan democracy, in the long run it became one of its main problems. Political parties and politicians became too comfortable within a system that secured them a place in government despite electoral results. This increased their level of autonomy, which in the long term transformed itself into impunity. Both parties became resistant to any political change. Moreover, as governors and mayors were named by the president, clientelism was at its peak during this period of territorial centralization. This political system was legalized and legitimized with the 1961 Constitution, and it was defined as a 'populist system of elite conciliation that imposed a system of negotiations, transactions and compromises' (Magdaleno 2013: 239).

From the time of the government of Rómulo Betancourt (AD, 1959–64) Venezuela began a process of consolidation of democracy. The 1968 elections were a turning point when Rafael Caldera from COPEI won the vote. This was the first alternation in power and the first opportunity to test the *Punto Fijo* accord. One of the journalists interviewed for this research pointed out that 'the *Punto Fijo* had political titans'. In the 1973 elections, Carlos Andrés Pérez won the presidency and the political party system seem to be consolidated (Rey 1998). This process of democratic consolidation has to be understood in its historical context. Magdaleno (2013) argues that the huge increase in oil revenues helped the governments from AD and COPEI to expand public expenditure and meet social demands. In 1972 the oil revenues were 7,884 million bolivars, in 1974 they reached 36,448 million; in 1980, 45,331 million, and in 1981, 70,886 million (ibid.). Oil revenues were around 70–80 per cent of the total public revenues (Romero 1996).

We suggest that the combination of high oil revenues and political stability explains the high degree of autonomy that the political parties acquired in Venezuela. In terms of political stability, the *Punto Fijo* accord guaranteed that AD and COPEI would be in government. There were no threats from other political actors. These two political parties became very powerful with a high degree of influence over domestic matters. There were no other political actors who could challenge their power (Crisp 1997).

If Argentina and Ecuador are examples of low institutionalization and Uruguay presents a degree of institutionalization that seems to balance the political system, then Venezuela, after 1958, shows an over-institutionalization of the political party system that gives parties and politicians a high degree of autonomy. In the case of Venezuela, we will go a step farther to suggest that in the long term the *Punto Fijo* coalition ensured the iron law of oligarchy, as explained by Robert Michels (1962). The elected were dominating the electors with a high degree of autonomy. Here, we argue that the degree of political parties' autonomy depends on the democratic quality of electoral competition. If electoral competition is weak, political parties increase their autonomy and capacity to ignore citizens and rules. The *Punto Fijo* in Venezuela gave parties a high degree of autonomy (Ellner 1988). The long-term consequences of the *Punto Fijo* pact were that AD and COPEI became over-autonomous, too powerful, and too corrupt. Politicians were so isolated that they did not spot the signs of popular discontent.

During the oil boom, the governments of Carlos Andrés Pérez (1974–79) and Luis Herrera Campins (1979–84) increased the public debt. In 1974, the external and internal debt totalled 10,176 million bolivars; in 1979 the total was 54,533 million, and in 1981 66,654 million (Romero 1996). By the end of the 1970s, Venezuela began to show signs of political and economic exhaustion: a highly indebted and oil-dependent economy managed by politicians who were gradually unable to maintain political consensus. The impact that oil had on Venezuelan politics has been analysed before (Karl 1986, 1995). Here we would like to emphasize that the AD and COPEI leadership was economically sustained by oil price increases, especially from 1973 (Magdaleno 2013). However, Corrales (2010) points out that from 1973 to 1983, the oil boom became an obstacle to any economic reform in Venezuela. Indeed, governments chose fiscal expansion as their main economic strategy, since economic opportunities were considered infinite during the price boom. However, once the international context changed, the Venezuelan governments were forced to amend their strategy. The external debt crisis that affected Latin America from 1982 and the end of the oil boom made it impossible to continue with the policies of fiscal expansion and redistribution of oil revenues.

In 1989, Carlos Andrés Pérez from AD won the elections with 52 per cent of the total vote. The COPEI candidate obtained 40 per cent of the vote, showing a strong polarization of the results. However, there were two political parties which were gaining in strength: Movimiento al Socialismo (MAS) and La Causa Radical. Both had been created in 1971 from divisions within the Communist Party, and, although in the presidential elections they received less than 5 per cent of the vote, in the regional elections they achieved better results, winning two governorships. AD obtained

39 per cent of the vote; COPEI, 31 per cent; and MAS, 17 per cent. This showed that political and territorial decentralization could end the monopoly of power shared by AD and COPEI (El País 1989). It was the first time, since 1958, that the domination of AD and COPEI was threatened.

The 1980s have been defined as the era of disillusion; many frustrations emerged since the Great Venezuela promised by Carlos Andrés Pérez in the 1970s never happened (Romero 1996; Magdaleno 2013). This could explain why, only three and a half weeks and after taking office, Carlos Andrés Pérez was confronted by the social revolt known as the *Caracazo*. In February 1989, Pérez increased the price of petrol and urban transport, which unleashed social unrest that ended with 276 dead. The *Caracazo* made evident the wide gap between politicians and citizens. Carlos Andrés Pérez was a strong leader, popular and populist, who had won the elections with more than 50 per cent of the vote, but after less than a month in government he became terribly unpopular. He had inherited a bankrupt country with a fiscal deficit of 9.4 per cent of GDP and the largest current-account deficit in Venezuelan history (Reid 2007). After Pérez's impeachment, Rafael Caldera won the 1993 elections with only 30 per cent of the total vote. After the collapse of the second-largest bank, Banco Latino, Caldera reintroduced Pérez's reform programme but under a different name: *Agenda Venezuela*.

It is relevant to ask why the economic reforms were strongly opposed in Venezuela when other Latin American countries, such as Argentina and Peru, implemented them. Magdaleno (2013) offers three reasons to explain this rejection. First, the 1970s and 1980s established a populist political culture based on the redistribution of oil revenues. Secondly, there was internal opposition from AD and COPEI to the economic reforms. Therefore, political actors were no longer able to achieve consensus, especially on economic strategy. Thirdly, Carlos Andrés Pérez was a very popular politician who overestimated his ability to implement an economic adjustment. A deteriorating economic situation with leaders who were unable to read citizens' demands and the need for political renewal were the precursor of the collapse of the *Punto Fijo* accord and its political stability.

We suggest that Venezuela is a case of over-institutionalization of the political party system with low, undemocratic, electoral competition that allows political parties to be autonomous. Through the *Punto Fijo*, the traditional parties themselves guaranteed their position in government. Thus, over-institutionalization can give parties a high degree of autonomy. While the emergence of the Frente Amplio in Uruguay benefited electoral competition by breaking the traditional equilibrium between Blancos and Colorados, in the long run the *Punto Fijo* accord in Venezuela provoked a deterioration of electoral competition (Tedesco and Diamint 2013). Owing to the appearance of a new political actor, the Frente Amplio, Uruguay avoided an over-institutionalization of its political party system and a deterioration in electoral competition. Venezuela did not. Here again we can see leadership from a collective perspective that, in this case, negatively led to the emergence of an autonomous, strong, leader. The *Punto Fijo* political class undermined the degree of representation and political competition, provoking a change of regime that deepened the undermining of democracy with the emergence of Hugo Chávez.

There are six main factors that should be considered to understand the emergence of Hugo Chávez in Venezuela. First, the political elite, rather than facing the challenges posed by the *Caracazo*, continued to be immersed in party politics and ignored, or misunderstood, citizens' demands. Secondly, governments from different political parties were no longer effectively dealing with economic problems, which eroded the legitimacy of state institutions and political parties. Thirdly, owing to the economic problems, AD and COPEI were undergoing internal crisis and a confrontation between them that undermined their political coalition. Fourthly, the traditional political parties were no longer able to channel social demands. Fifthly, Hugo Chávez understood the *Caracazo* message and citizens' rejection of austerity measures and the neoliberal agenda. Lastly, he offered a very simple discourse that blamed political parties and politicians for the economic crisis.

Hugo Chávez was able to build power and autonomy outside the old party system. The control of the armed forces and the oil rents together with the creation of an extensive social programme to improve the quality of life of urban and rural marginal sectors allowed him to concentrate power in his hands for fourteen years. His government was legitimized, and his autonomy increased thanks to many victories in elections and referendums.

The post-crisis scenario

The story of Hugo Chávez is well known. Chávez was a military officer who, in 1982, formed a movement within the armed forces known as Ejército Bolivariano Revolucionario-200 (Bolivarian Revolutionary Army-200), later called Movimiento Bolivariano Revolucionario-200 (Revolutionary Bolivarian Movement-200). He emerged as a political figure with the attempted military coup of February 1992. He was imprisoned and released in 1994 by President Rafael Caldera. McCoy (1999: 67) emphasizes that Chávez was eligible to run for office because he was never convicted and thus 'he quietly began to build an impressive campaign throughout the country'. In 1997 he created his own political party, Movimiento Quinta República (MVR, Fifth Republic Movement). He won the elections in 1998 with 56 per cent of the total vote.

One of our respondents stated that this election marked the end of an era. Venezuelans were angry with the political elite of the *Punto Fijo* and Chávez was offering them a transformation. A union leader explained: 'Hugo Chávez was a product of the end of a historical period in Venezuela'. Sixty-two per cent of our respondents agreed that the president had a high approval rating because citizens believed that he cared about them, and especially about the poorest. In our interviews, most of the political opponents recognized Chávez's charisma and his ability to communicate and to talk to the underprivileged. One of our respondents argued that Chávez was able to give the poor a role as a political actor.

In his presidential oath he proclaimed: 'I swear before God and my people that upon this moribund Constitution I will drive forth the necessary democratic transformations so that the new republic will have a Carta Magna befitting these new times' (Marcano and Barrera 2007). Chávez was clear from the very beginning that he would transform state institutions. Indeed, in order to concentrate power in his hands and to create a system of presidentialist domination, Chávez started a process that would create new institutions and transform old ones to eliminate the system of checks and balances. It was the beginning of a period that would concentrate power in the hands of the president, undermining the rule of law.

In order to change the Constitution, Chávez called for a public referendum to form a Constitutional Assembly. The referendum took place on 25 April 1999 and Chávez's proposal won with 88 per cent of the vote. In August of that year, the Constitutional Assembly proclaimed itself sovereign, replacing the Congress that had been elected in 1998 and the Supreme Court. This was the beginning of a long process that entailed the modification of the balance of power between the legislative, the executive and the judiciary. The Assembly gave itself powers to dismiss state officials it considered corrupt. The Constitutional Assembly replaced the members of the Supreme Tribunal of Justice, the National Electoral Council and the Attorney General. Finally the Assembly wrote a new Constitution. In December 1999 there was a referendum to adopt the Constitution, which was approved by 72 per cent of the vote.

The new law was 'the most heavily presidentialist constitution in contemporary Latin America' (Corrales and Penfold 2007: 186). It included more rights and protection for indigenous people and women and established the rights to education, housing, healthcare and food. It increased the presidential term from five to six years with a single re-election and allowed people to recall presidents by referendum. The Congress became a unicameral body, the National Assembly. The president had the power to legislate and to call for public referendums without support from the Assembly. The military obtained more powers and a role in the government, on the grounds that they have to ensure public order and aid national development. The political parties could not receive public financing. Finally, the executive also gained control over the National Electoral Council, which governs electoral affairs.

With the new Constitution and the new Assembly, President Chávez dismantled the old political regime and began a process of power concentration in the executive. He became a firm power usurper with all the features that we defined: he challenged the rules, polarized society and maximized his power (see Table 2.5).

One of the instruments that Chávez used to usurp power from other institutions was the so called *Leyes Habilitantes* (Habilitating Laws). These laws, approved by the National Assembly, gave power to the president to legislate. Thus, the president took over the role of the legislative. In 1999, Chávez asked for approval of a *Ley Habilitante* that allowed him to legislate by decree. The Assembly sanctioned the law for a six-month period. During this period Chávez approved fifty-three decrees, mainly on economic and financial issues.

In 1999, Chávez launched Plan Bolivar 2000. Around 70,000 members of the armed forces would help to repair roads, schools and hospitals and offer free medical care and vaccinations. The Plan Bolivar gave a new role to the armed forces and was the antecedent of the *Misiones* (community-based social plans).

Three main pillars would be developed by Chávez to increase and maintain his power: the *Misiones*, elections and referendums. One of our respondents explained that there were many elections and referendums but participation was low. He argued that citizens felt incorporated into politics through Chávez and did not feel the need to vote.

In 2000 Venezuela held elections in July and December to elect the president, members of the National Assembly, governors, mayors and city councillors. Chávez was re-elected with almost 60 per cent of the vote. In the National Assembly, his supporters won 101 seats out of 165. In November 2000, the Assembly passed another *Ley Habilitante* which gave the president the power to legislate throughout one year. In this period forty-nine decrees were passed on issues pertaining to natural resources, especially legislation regarding land and hydrocarbons. In 2001 the government introduced a new hydrocarbon law to increase its control over the oil industry. They increased the royalties and introduced the formation of mixed companies whereby PDVSA, the national oil company, would have joint control with private companies over the oil industry. By 2006, all the agreements with private companies were controlled by PDVSA. The president was not only usurping power from other institutions of the state but also from private companies.

After the attempted coup in 2002, and thanks to an oil windfall, Chávez launched the *Misiones*, which helped him to increase his power by captivating the hearts of millions of poor Venezuelans. The *Misiones* helped him to win the 2004 recall referendum. He won 59 per cent of the vote. After this victory, he used his majority in the National Assembly to change twelve judges in the Supreme Court. While the *Leyes Habilitantes* helped him to overrule the legislative, the change of twelve judges was a clear move to neutralize any type of independence or opposition in the judiciary. This was another tool that allowed Chávez to usurp power.

The *Misiones* became a pillar of Chávez's power and increasing popularity. Sixty-seven per cent of our respondents in Caracas defined clientelism as an exchange of benefits for votes; 93 per cent agreed that the *Misiones* were a clientelist tool; 43 per cent believed that clientelism persists because it is functional to a specific form of political domination and 28 per cent argued that clientelist policies replace the state when it fails to provide public services. Clientelism is criticized, but 57 per cent of our respondents argued that it is very effective when the aim is to accumulate power. However, in unequal countries such as Venezuela, social policies are crucial to improve income distribution. According to ECLAC, in 1998 49 per cent of Venezuelans were considered to be poor (CEPAL 2012). In 2011, the percentage of poor people in the country had decreased to 27 per cent. All our respondents said that in the case of a Mesa de la Unidad Democrática (MUD, Democratic Unity Roundtable) government, the *Misiones* should be continued. The political abuse of social policies, which could be considered as clientelism, does not erase the need to establish measures to change the situation of the poorest.

In October 2004 there were regional elections. Chávez's supporters won twenty-one out of twenty-three state governments and more than 90 per cent of the municipalities (Corrales and Penfold 2007). By 2005 the opposition was in disarray. Most of the opposition decided to boycott the National Assembly elections in December 2005. Consequently Chávez's partisans won all the seats in the Assembly. In the 2006 presidential elections, Chávez won with 63 per cent of the vote. At this time, he created the PSUV, which was an umbrella organization that encompassed all leftist political parties that supported the Chávez regime. By 2007, 5.7 million people belonged to the PSUV (Cannon 2009). He argued that this umbrella organization would have a bottom-up structure to help the emergence of new leaders, but in reality this did not happen and the PSUV became a mere follower of a strong leader (ibid.).

With or without the PSUV, Chávez was a great communicator and a highly popular president. One of our respondents emphasized that Chávez was able to speak in very simple terms and his message was clear to anybody. Another respondent suggested that he was a postmodern *caudillo*: a military, Christian strong man.

In January 2007, Chávez asked again for the approval of a *Ley Habilitante*. He got it for eighteen months. This law allowed him to legislate on energy; economic, social and financial issues; tax reforms; state institutions and popular participation. He sanctioned fifty-nine laws during this exceptional period.

After the 2006 victory, Chávez was expanding his power and stepping up his persecution of political opponents. The government would not renew the licence of RCTV, the biggest opposition television station. A law was passed to make it very difficult for NGOs to receive foreign donations. Finally, 'those on the list of the 3.4 million people who signed the petition for the recall referendum found themselves liable to be sacked from government jobs and denied public services, from passports to loans and contracts' (Reid 2007: 172).

There was another referendum in December 2007 to reform sixty-nine articles of the Constitution. The amendments encompassed indefinite re-election for the president and all elective officials, changing the presidential term from six years to seven, the militarization of the country with the president able to create Strategic Zones in any area of the Venezuelan territory and suspend democratic rights, the creation of new forms of popular participation, such as *Consejos del Poder Popular* or *Células Sociales*, and the establishment of a socialist democracy. The changes were rejected by 50.65 per cent of the vote, which showed the degree of polarization that Venezuela achieved during the Chávez regime. This was the first time that Chávez had lost an election. Since 1999, he had won eleven votes in elections and referendums.

After this defeat, the opposition camp gained new momentum. The Mesa de la Unidad Democrática (MUD, Democratic Unity Roundtable) was established in 2008 and by 2010 included fifty political parties from the centre, centre-left and centre-right. The main unifying factor of the MUD was its opposition to Hugo Chávez. The main member parties were Democratic Action and COPEI, the two parties which dominated Venezuelan politics from 1959 to 1999. Other parties that joined the MUD were the Movement for Socialism (Movimiento al Socialismo), Radical Cause (Causa Radical), the Red Flag Party (Partido Bandera Roja), Project Venezuela (Proyecto Venezuela), A New Era (Un Nuevo Tiempo), Justice First (Primero Justicia) and PODEMOS. Despite the collapse of the political party system and President Chávez's assaults, a large number of the MUD still believed that political parties were relevant for democracy. Indeed, 49 per cent of our respondents agreed that political parties should be the pillars of a democratic political regime, and 24 per cent believed that they are the main channels for citizens' demands; but 11 per cent were more negative, seeing political parties as mere tools for the accumulation of power. However, as Chávez's discourse has been very successful in presenting the political parties as inefficient and corrupt, even young politicians were careful when debating the role of political parties.

Under the Constitution, President Chávez could not stand for election again so he called for another referendum in February 2009 to abolish the two-term limit for all public offices. His proposal won with 54 per cent of the total vote. He had secured a chance of indefinite re-election.

In 2010 there was another *Ley Habilitante* for eighteen months as a response to violent storms in the country. During these eighteen months, fifty-four laws were passed. Chávez asked for special powers to legislate on infrastructure, transport, public services, housing, development and urban and rural land. He was also able to

legislate on citizen security, national defence, international cooperation and economic issues.

By 1999, President Chávez had achieved complete control of all
the institutions of the state. As one of our respondents put it, 'the
executive had kidnapped all the powers of the state'. Chávez was
also breaking the boundaries between the president and the state.

In the September 2010 election for the National Assembly the MUD
won around 47 per cent of the vote nationally. This new situation, with
the emergence of a political opponent, changed dramatically when in
June 2011 Chávez announced from Cuba that he had cancer.

Since the 2007 defeat, the political scenario in Venezuela had
changed. The opposition was becoming stronger and Chávez was
weaker because of his illness. The October 2012 elections were very
different from previous ones under the Chávez regime. The president was ill and the opposition was united. The MUD held open
primaries in February 2012. Around three million citizens voted in
the primaries and Henrique Capriles, from Primero Justicia, won
with 63 per cent of the vote. In October, Chávez won the presidential elections with 55 per cent of the vote. Capriles received 44 per cent.
Chávez became extremely ill and was unable to take office in January
2013. He died in March and new elections were held in April. Nicolás
Maduro, Chávez's elected successor, won 50.61 per cent of the vote
and Henrique Capriles won 49.12 per cent.

No doubt Chávez fundamentally changed Venezuelan politics in
the short and in the long term. He also changed how political leadership is understood, and this is the issue that we analyse in the next
section.

Conceptualizing political leadership

Although our respondents opposed President Chávez, all of them
agreed that he was a charismatic leader. They all praised his ability to communicate with his followers, his capacity to engage with

the underprivileged, his talent for speaking for a long time and his powerful image. They also pointed to his aggressive speeches and his authoritarian and paternalistic style. They emphasized that Chávez created a leadership style that was difficult to emulate and impossible to forget. Most of them agreed that the new, younger leaders who were emerging in the MUD were trying to follow Chávez's style in one way or another. For instance, one of our respondents explained that Chávez concentrated his discourse at the micro level, talking with his followers about problems in their neighbourhood, their local school or clinic. The younger generation of leaders was doing the same, leaving aside discussions about economic strategy, the problems of infrastructure and urban violence.

Chávez was defined as an omnipotent, charismatic leader. He was paternalistic and caring to some and authoritarian and arrogant to others. He polarized society, provoking love and hatred. One of our respondents suggested that Chávez created a reality show; he sacked ministers on television, sang, made jokes, got angry with his political opponents and insulted the United States. Every time he appeared on television, he put on a show. He seduced his followers. He was a politician and an entertainer. He transformed the image of the political leader. From the time Chávez appeared on the political scene, Venezuelans were seduced into a personality cult. His followers were charmed and enchanted by him. Many of our respondents agree that Chávez has became a messianic figure.

His type of leadership had two contrasting effects. For his followers he was a caring father, fighting for their interests, protecting them and providing them with goods and services through the *Misiones*. He represented the majority of Venezuelans; he was considered one of them. He understood their situation, spoke their language, taught them about their rights and made them feel important. For his opponents, he was an authoritarian, populist, clientelist president whose main aim was to concentrate power in his hands. 'Chávez wins in all games where he polarizes and confronts,' said an opposition leader. However, all of our respondents stated that he could not be considered a dictator. Although there were some human rights violations, persecutions of political opponents, a reduction in the freedom of expression and civil liberties, our interviewees pointed out that Chávez was not like the Latin American dictators of the 1970s. In fact, 93 per cent of our respondents agreed that the 1999 Constitution expanded human rights guarantees, improving women's rights and indigenous rights. Nevertheless, 87 per cent stated that there was discrimination on political grounds, and permanent attacks on the independence of the judiciary and on the freedom of the press.

There was also consensus among our interviewees that the emergence of Chávez provoked a renewal of political elites. He also transformed the understanding of politics and of leadership. The interviews described a type of leader who was democratic, legitimate, charismatic, a polarizer and omnipotent, clientelist and authoritarian. It was a complex characterization which combined democracy and authoritarianism. Indeed, Chávez organized many elections and referendums while manipulating the institutions of the state, especially the system of checks and balances.

In our typology he was a power usurper. Chávez was simultaneously a rule challenger, a polarizer and a power maximizer. He was democratically elected and used elections and referendums to transform state institutions and increase his power. The *Leyes Habilitantes* were a tool to usurp power from the legislative. Changing the judges of the Supreme Court in 2004 undermined the power and the independence of the judiciary. When he lost the 2007 referendum, he called for a new one in 2009 to approve indefinite re-election. He was using referendums and elections to concentrate power in his hands. President Chávez also employed clientelism and populism to increase his personal power. This was very evident in the establishment of the *Misiones*. Indeed, in 2003 his popularity was decreasing and the *Misiones* provided a huge boost.

A charismatic leader, a polarizer, a rule challenger and a power maximizer, Hugo Chávez displays all the features of a power usurper. However, we would like to suggest that the undermining of civil liberties and the freedom of the press was not extreme. There was a combination of persecution of opponents and an important degree of freedom to criticize the government.

Regarding the role of the political parties, all of our respondents were very cautious about it. Hugo Chávez, like Rafael Correa in Ecuador, had been very successful in his attacks on political parties, especially AD and COPEI. However, as mentioned above, 49 per cent of our respondents agreed that political parties are key to a democratic political regime, 24 per cent believed that parties are the main channels for social demands and, from a more negative perspective, 11 per cent defined political parties as mere tools for the accumulation of power.

One of the unintended consequences of the *Punto Fijo* accord was the discrediting of the main political parties, AD and COPEI. According to 75 per cent of our respondents the new parties, such as Movement for Socialism (Movimiento al Socialismo), Radical Cause (Causa Radical), the Red Flag Party (Partido Bandera Roja), Project Venezuela (Proyecto Venezuela), A New Era (Un Nuevo Tiempo), Justice First (Primero Justicia) and PODEMOS, had a responsibility to show that they could be different. One of the main objectives of the February 2012 primaries was to demonstrate that. We conducted interviews with young leaders from all of these new political groupings and they all agreed that to defeat Chávez, unity under the umbrella of the MUD was necessary. These political parties did not have strong ideological differences. Their aim was to renovate politics and to organize the opposition to Chávez. As one young leader stated, 'what unites us is our opposition to the president'.

In the interviews Chávez was also characterized as a polarizing leader. Here we would like to reiterate that all our respondents

were from the opposition movements and considered Chávez the
main problem in Venezuelan politics. Under his presidency, the
country became highly polarized. He provoked love and hatred.
Eighty-three per cent of our respondents argued that Chávez
was always able to deepen and take advantage of the polarization
because a majority of Venezuelans supported his policies. One of
our respondents emphasized that he also created fear among his
supporters by proclaiming that the opposition would dismantle the
Misiones.

President Chávez, argued most of our respondents, became the
only voice in politics in Venezuela. His leadership was understood
as direct, since there were no intermediaries between him and
his people. In the eyes of our respondents, the PSUV had never
attempted to become a communication channel between the leader
and his followers.

His charismatic leadership was screened on TV. He made politics a big show with his TV programme *Aló Presidente*, which was
broadcast every Sunday from 11 a.m. until he was done talking.
Cameras followed him around the country, showing the results of
his Bolivarian Revolution and his power. Enrique Krauze (Nolan
2012) pointed out that '*Aló Presidente* gives Venezuelans at least the
appearance of contact with power, through his verbal and visual
presence, which may be welcomed by people who have spent most
of their lives being ignored'. Eighty-seven per cent of our respondents agreed that Chávez's innovation was the economic, social and
political inclusion of millions of underprivileged citizens. This was
also his main contribution – the young leaders from the new political organizations recognized in the interviews that the poorest of
the poor could no longer be ignored by Venezuelan politicians.
Chávez had politically activated the poor sectors of society and
highlighted the African and indigenous roots of Venezuela's population (Trinkunas 2002: 42). This initiated the establishment of a
sacred relationship between Chávez and his followers. One of our

respondents argued that Venezuelans understand leadership with a religious touch.

In our interviews the conceptualization of leadership was defined by Chávez's style. The political opposition expressed the opinion that a leader has to have charisma, strong personality and a paternalistic attitude. However, 86 per cent of our respondents mentioned the Chilean Concertación as the ideal type of political leadership. The young leaders of the opposition in Venezuela preferred collective political leadership, criticizing Chávez's concentration of power. Ninety-two per cent of the interviewees agreed that one of the main problems of Chávez's style of leadership is that the president becomes the only guarantor of the political model. They also stated that they wanted to find a happy medium between strong leaders who could oppose Chávez and a collective leadership to avoid an extreme concentration of power.

Based on our interviews, we suggest that the collapse of the *Punto Fijo* accord together with the discrediting of the traditional political parties helped the emergence of a strong leader who was able to transform the institutions of the state and politics. Chávez is an extreme example of a power usurper. In a context of over-institutionalization of the political party system, an economic crisis opened the door to outsiders and anti-systemic leaders. In our research, Venezuela, Ecuador and Argentina indicate that these situations help the emergence of power usurpers. If the economic crisis is reversed and a period of economic growth (thanks to an oil or soya boom) follows, the probability of having a power usurper increases.

The power usurper is a leader who has three main features: he is a rule challenger, a polarizer and a power maximizer. He is a rule challenger because he manipulates constitutional or electoral instruments. In the case of Chávez, he changed the Constitution and the electoral system to concentrate power in his hands and undermine any opposition from the legislative or the judiciary. Through the four *Leyes Habilitantes*, Chávez usurped power from the legislative.

Chávez used clientelism and populism to increase his personal power, undermined civil liberties, undermined press freedom and horizontal accountability.

The power usurper is also a polarizer. As mentioned before, Chávez increased the polarization of society. He was intolerant of his opponents and refused to share the decision-making process. Chávez took advantage of the failures of the *Punto Fijo* to discredit traditional political parties. Even when in 2007 there was a new student movement which opposed Chávez's referendum, he referred to them as 'the children of the old regime'. Our respondents from the new political organizations argued that it has taken a monumental effort to overcome the bad reputation of the parties.

Concentration of power is one of the main aims of a power usurper, which illustrates the third feature of being a power maximizer. The leader has a high capacity to ignore the rules and citizens' demands. He undermines political opposition, perpetuates himself in power and believes that he is more important than democracy. Usually, the power usurper is highly ideological. Through his ideology, Chávez motivated and inspired millions of Venezuelans. A young leader from an opposition party told us how significant it was to see previously excluded citizens holding the Constitution as if it were the Bible. Chávez was without doubt a great orator and he convinced his followers that he cared about each of them. However, he also used his speeches to confront his political opponents, whom he considered his enemies. A traditional politician who was a member of COPEI recognized Chávez's ability to discredit political parties and political opponents.

In the interviews, the Venezuelan political leaders described Chávez as an extreme power usurper. It became clear that the president had rewritten the concept of leader. We wanted to explore how political leadership, independently of Chávez's style, was understood by our respondents, so we asked them to explain what type of political leader the MUD would offer. All our respondents from the different political parties that were included in the MUD agreed that leadership should be collective with political parties as its main pillars. One representative said, 'parties have been strengthened. People understood the importance of having these mechanisms of political mediation.' After so many years of strong leaders, they suggested that Venezuela was ready for a different kind of leadership. The example of the Concertación in Chile was mentioned in 87 per cent of the interviews. However, they also recognized the need to find a charismatic leader; 92 per cent argued that a Chávez political opponent should be young and charismatic. They also stated that a government from the opposition should continue with the *Misiones*. As one of our respondents explained, 'the *Misiones* are now a need in Venezuela'.

Despite the fact that most of our respondents gave priority to the strengthening of political parties, they also pointed out that whoever emerges from the MUD should be a strong leader. One of the young politicians of a new political party said, 'most of the people will vote for the strongest leader'. However, they also emphasized the importance of building consensus and dialogue to mark a crucial difference with the Chávez government.

A charismatic, strong, young leader supported by empowered political parties and a promoter of dialogue and consensus was the ideal leader, according to our respondents. Their main aim was to reform politics and to depolarize society.

We would suggest that in our typology such a leader is closer to an ambivalent democrat or a democracy enhancer. After so many years of a power usurper in government, our respondents argued for the building or reinforcement of democratic institutions, the promotion of horizontal accountability and respect for democratic rights and civil liberties. They aimed to establish consensus so that they could be considered bridge builders. Finally, they expressed the need to respect the limits imposed by state institutions. It is important to highlight that these were their goals. Whether they follow them strictly if one day they are in government, or whether they continue to exercise a leadership more similar to our model of the power usurper, is beyond our analysis since they are still outside the Palacio de Miraflores.

Conclusion

The collapse of the party system opens the door to power usurpers. In the case of Venezuela, Hugo Chávez was the consequence of the failures of the *Punto Fijo*. However, it is essential to emphasize that Chávez was unique. He was extremely charismatic. Above all, he was a great communicator and understood his citizens' demands.

Our study indicates that in order to understand the emergence of Chávez it is essential to examine the slow deterioration of the traditional party system. This does not mean that the collapse of a party system necessarily brings in a charismatic leader, but it does make the appearance of a power usurper more likely.

Having analysed our five cases studies, our aim is now to present our general conclusions by answering the following questions: In what way does our typology help to understand political leadership? Does it help to advance the study of leaders? Does it say something about the democratic qualities of the leaders?

CHAPTER 6

Rethinking Political Leadership

We began this research because we wanted to discover the impact that political leaders have on the quality of democracy. As the research was developing, different questions arose: Why has the return to democracy not changed the tendency to generate strong leaders? Why did recent presidential crises end with the emergence of strong leaders? Can domestic conditions explain the emergence of different types of leader?

We believed that the key to answering these questions was the leaders themselves. Using material from 285 interviews, we argue that the emergence of different types of leader is intrinsically related to the political context, and especially to the degree of institution-alization of the political party system. We observe that it is also related to the degree of electoral competition and the autonomy that a leader can establish, free of other political actors. This situation promotes the emergence of a soft power usurper or a power usurper. Argentina, Ecuador and Venezuela show that the logic behind this scenario is that the concentration of power is considered necessary to secure political stability.

Leaders in Uruguay and Colombia present a different picture. They tell us that if parties are strongly institutionalized, then leaders find it more difficult to gain autonomy. Indeed, Uruguay in particular shows that institutionalized political parties do have power to control and limit leaders' autonomy. In Colombia, Álvaro Uribe's aspirations to continue in government met effective resistance from the judiciary.

In post-crisis scenarios countries can fall into a political trap: Argentina, Ecuador and Venezuela show that opponents can get rid of bad presidents but have been unable to make sure that the newcomer will be any better. We have considered the question of why Latin American voters have often ejected bad, undemocratic leaders from office, but then voted in new leaders who turn out to be just as bad for democratic quality. The answer lies in the state of political parties. Our research shows that the deterioration of political parties undermines the possibility of training democratic leaders and the tools needed to prevent undemocratic leaders taking power. Political parties are key in the formation and monitoring of new generations of democratic leaders.

The cases of Argentina, Ecuador and Venezuela help us to explore why the return to democracy has not changed Latin America's tendency to generate strong leaders (soft power usurpers or power usurpers). Rather than a democratization of political parties, what happened during the 1980s and the 1990s was that parties became increasingly disconnected from citizens' demands. They became almost redundant, challenged by powerful leaders.

We observe that in post-crisis scenarios, the deterioration of the political party system allows presidents to disempower institutions in order to empower themselves. In this context soft power usurpers and power usurpers can prevail and the quality of democracy declines.

The combination of strong leaders and weak institutions erodes the pillars of liberal democracy. Our respondents in Argentina, Ecuador and Venezuela seem to suggest that citizens look for powerful leaders to compensate for the weakness of political parties. In the long term, power usurpers do not have the incentives to empower institutions that could control or monitor their activities. In Argentina, Ecuador and Venezuela leaders seem to be more important than democracy. They have a striking capacity to ignore rules and citizens' demands.

With the exceptions of those in Uruguay and Colombia, the majority of our respondents thought of power as hard power; of democracy as concentration of power; and of leadership as strength. In Uruguay, our respondents talked in terms of soft power, power distribution among the different institutions of the state and of collective leadership. In Colombia, strong political leaders have been effectively controlled and monitored by democratic institutions.

In Uruguay political parties and citizens seem to be as important as democracy. In Colombia, even in a context of political violence, institutions seem to be as important as democracy. In Uruguay and Colombia politicians are held accountable by their parties and state institutions – and their autonomy is limited.

The value of our typology

Theoretically, the book emphasizes that the study of political leaders needs to be contextualized. Leaders are a historical product. However, they are also able to transform the context. They are both makers and products of political history. Thus, in order to understand their emergence and their legacy, the research has to be contextualized. The book suggests that a combination of domestic conditions and leaders' ability is key to understanding political leadership.

The contextualization explained the different institutional settings that promoted the emergence of different types of leaders. Most analysis of leaders in Latin America presents general perspectives that highlight the strongman or *caudillo*. Here we propose a more sophisticated approach. Our typology uses factors related to: political context; leaders' ability to lead; and leaders' impact on the quality of democracy. It is based on three dimensions: the leader's attitude towards the rule of law; whether the leader seeks consensus or provokes polarization; and the methods the leaders uses to increase power.

This is a theoretical construction, an ideal type which differs from real-life cases. The typology is not an end in itself. It is a tool to explore and compare different types of leaders, how and why they emerge and their impact on the quality of democracy.

Our typology is not inductive. First we analysed the political scenarios. Secondly, we conducted the interviews. Thirdly, we looked for trends, relations, differences and similarities. Finally, we articulated the typology.

The qualitative analysis derived from the interviews helped us to construct the different types of leader based on three factors: their relation with the rule of law, their ability to build consensus or promote polarization and their style of building power. These three factors implicitly show the democratic quality of the different leadership types since they are based on the relations that leaders establish with a range of political elements: the Constitution, electoral laws, institutions of the state, civil liberties, horizontal accountability, polarization, tolerance, autonomy, power sharing, citizens, political opposition and personal power. In this sense, the typology provides a comprehensive framework in which examine the democratic quality of leaders. Here lies the originality of our contribution, namely that we characterize democratic leaders through their actions. Does the leader work with his cabinet? Does he listen to the opposition? Does he manipulate norms to perpetuate himself in government? Is he tolerant?

We suggest that our typology encapsulates the components to distinguish the degree of democraticness of political leaders and offers four ideal types which include extreme and moderate. We hope that this typology offers guidelines for how leaders' political influence can also be studied in other parts of the world.

This book also offers ideas about conducting research on political leaders. We have described the difficulties encountered in basing our research on interviews with politicians. The current debate about quantitative or qualitative research influenced the design of the research project from the beginning. We are aware that our decision to privilege the qualitative research might be questioned. However, we argue that the originality of this research comes from the in-depth analysis of 285 interviews with politicians and the comparative perspective.

We hope that the book presents some questions that could become the subject of broader research agendas. However, our hope is also that leaders and citizens become more interested in this type of research because they have the key to provoke change. Leaders can use our typology as a guide to become democratic enhancers. For citizens it can be a tool to demand accountability. Scholars can consider it as a step to help expand the study of democratic leadership.

After many years working on leaders we have mixed feelings about the future of democracy. Politicians have been able to offer us a comprehensive diagnosis of the impact of leaders on the quality of democracy. However, very few were prepared to suggest ideas for democratizing politics and leaders. They seem to be more concerned about the short term, elections and their continuation in office than the long-lasting reward of building a more democratic society.

List of Interviews

ARGENTINA

1. **2 November 2009. José Pampuro.** National Senator for the province of Buenos Aires (2005–11), Victory Front (Frente para la Victoria, PJ).
2. **25 November 2009. Marcelo Stubrin.** Ex-National Deputy (1983–85, 1985–89 and 1995–99) for the Radical Civic Union (Unión Cívica Radical, UCR).
3. **4 December 2009. Graciela Fernández Meijide.** Ex-National Deputy for the City of Buenos Aires (1993–95).
4. **4 December 2009. Carlos Snopek.** National Deputy for Jujuy (2005–09).
5. **9 December 2009. Federico Storani.** Ex-National Deputy for the province of Buenos Aires (1983–85, 1985–89, 1993–97, 1997–99, 2003–07).
6. **9 December 2009. Graciela Giannettasio.** National Deputy for the province of Buenos Aires (2007–11).
7. **10 December 2009. Vilma Ibarra.** National Deputy for the City of Buenos Aires (2007–11).
8. **11 December 2009. Héctor Recalde.** National Deputy for the province of Buenos Aires (2005–09).
9. **1 February 2010. José Luis Machinea.** Ex-Minister of Economy and Finance (December 1999–March 2001).
10. **16 February 2010. Héctor Flores.** National Deputy for Buenos Aires (2007–11) for the Civic Coalition (Coalición Cívica, CC).
11. **26 February 2010. Carlos Álvarez.** Ex-Vice-President (December 1999, October 2000).
12. **8 March 2010. Jesús Rodríguez.** Secretary General of the National Committee of the Radical Civic Union (Unión Cívica Radical, UCR). Ex-National Deputy (1983–87, 1987–91, 1993–97, 1999–2003).

13. **16 March 2010. Marcos Peña.** Secretary General of Buenos Aires City Government (Propuesta Republicana, PRO).
14. **18 March 2010. Héctor Álvaro.** National Deputy for Mendoza (2007–11) for the Citizen Collaboration Party. Founder of Popular Commitment in Mendoza.
15. **23 March 2010. Margarita Stolbizer.** National Deputy for the province of Buenos Aires (2009–13), for the Generation for National Togetherness (Generación para un Encuentro Nacional, GEN). President and founder of GEN.
16. **25 March 2010. Adrián Pérez.** National Deputy for the City of Buenos Aires (2003–07, 2007–11) for the Civic Coalition (Coalición Cívica, CC).
17. **26 March 2010. Enrique Nosiglia.** Ex-Minister of the Interior (1987–89).
18. **29 March 2010. Cecilia Merchán.** National Deputy for Cordoba (2007–11) for the Free Movement of the South (Movimiento Libres del Sur).
19. **29 March 2010. Diego Kravetz.** Legislator for the City of Buenos Aires for the Victory Front (Frente para la Victoria) (2003–07, 2007–11).
20. **5 April 2010. Gabriela Michetti.** National Deputy for the City of Buenos Aires (2009–13) for Propuesta Republicana, PRO.
21. **6 April 2010. Liliana Fellner.** National Senator for Jujuy (2005–11). Victory Front (Frente para la Victoria).
22. **6 April 2010. Cristian Gribaudo.** National Deputy for the province of Buenos Aires (2007–11). Propuesta Republicana, PRO.
23. **3 June 2010. Rubén Giustiniani.** National Senator for Santa Fe (2003–09, 2009–15). Socialist Party (Partido Socialista).
24. **8 June 2010. Eduardo Torres.** National Senator for Misiones (2007–11). Renewal Front (Frente Renovador).
25. **11 June 2010. María Eugenia Estenssoro.** National Senator for the City of Buenos Aires (2007–13). Civic Coalition (Coalición Cívica).
26. **5 July 2010. Rossana Bertone.** National Deputy for Tierra del Fuego (2001–05, 2005–09, 2009–13). Victory Front (Frente para la Victoria).
27. **8 July 2010. Martín Sabbatella.** National Deputy for Buenos Aires (2009–13).
28. **4 December 2009.** Santiago Leiras. Academic.
29. **7 December 2009. Juan Carlos Torre.** Professor and researcher at the Torcuato di Tella University – Department of Political Science and International Relations.
30. **11 February 2010. Hugo Yasky.** General Secretary of the Workers' Central of the Republic of Argentina (Central de Trabajadores de la República Argentina, CTA).
31. **12 February 2010. Monseñor Jorge Pedro Casaretto.** Bishop of San Isidro. President of Social Pastoral Care of Argentina (Pastoral Social Argentina).
32. **18 February 2010. Carlos de la Vega.** President of the Argentine Chamber of Commerce (Cámara Argentina de Comercio, CAC).
33. **25 February 2010. Mauro González.** President of the Federation of Young Entrepreneurs of Argentina (Federación Argentina de Jóvenes Empresarios, FEDAJE).

34. **3 March 2010. Susana Rueda.** Ex-Secretary General of the CGT (2003–04), Secretary for Institutional Relations and Policy at the ATSA Santa Fe.

35. **26 March 2010. Enrique Mantilla.** President of the Chamber of Exporters of Argentina (Cámara Argentina de Exportadores, CERA). Winner of the Konex Prize for Business Leader of the Year 2008.

36. **11 December 2009. Diana Maffia.** Deputy for the City of Buenos Aires (2007–11). Academic Coordinator of the Hannah Arendt Institute. Civic Coalition (Coalición Cívica).

37. **8 February 2010. Ramiro Etchegaray.** Head of the Buenos Aires office of the Contemporaneous Foundation (Fundación Contemporánea).

38. **8 February 2010. Martín Boccacci.** Coordinator of Strategic Thinking at the Contemporaneous Foundation (Fundación Contemporánea).

39. **9 February 2010. Camilo Vedia.** Moisés Lebensohn Institute of Thinking. Radical Youth (Juventud Radical).

40. **15 February 2010. Ramiro Tagliaferro.** Provincial Deputy for Buenos Aires (2007–11). Propuesta Republicana, PRO.

41. **23 March 2010. Juan González.** Alternative Popular University (Rosario university grouping). Secretary for policy training for the Rosario Peronist Youth.

42. **25 March 2010. Victoria Buratti.** Secretary for Education and Training of the Digital PJ.

43. **29 March 2010. Roberto Magliano.** Head of the Policy Formation Programme at the Juan Perón Institute of Higher Studies.

44. **30 March 2010. Nicolás Fernández Arroyo.** Director of the Municipal Leader Programme, Centre for Public Policy Implementation for Equity and Growth (Centro de Implementación de Políticas Públicas para la Equidad y el Crecimiento, CIPPEC).

45. **31 March 2010. Carlos Rizzuti.** Vice-President of the Civil Association for Popular Studies (Asociación Civil de Estudios Populares, ACEP).

46. **31 March 2010. Marcelo Ferreira.** Coordinator of I-Gen. (Institute of Studies for a New Generation).

47. **31 March 2010. Eduardo Beltrán.** Coordinator of the PROFIM-ICDA at the Catholic University of Cordoba and the Konrad Adenauer Foundation.

48. **8 April 2010. Silvina Viazzi.** Coordinator of Training for the Argentine Productive Movement (Movimiento Productivo Argentino, MPA).

49. **18 May 2010. Alan Clutterbuck.** Managing Council for the Policy Action Network Movement (Movimiento Red de Acción Política, RAP).

50. **18 May 2010. Paula Montoya.** Managing Council for the Policy Action Network Movement (Movimiento Red de Acción Política, RAP).

51. **27 May 2010. Martín Galanternik.** Founder and Executive Director of MINU. Member of the board of the Federal Youth Platform of Argentina.

52. **27 May 2010. Ilaina Rabbat.** Member of the Latin American School for Young Social Action (Escuela Latinoamericana para la Actoría Social Juvenil, ELASJ).

53. **1 June 2010. Alicia Ciciliani.** Secretary of the Centre for Municipal and Social Studies (Centro de Estudios Municipales y Sociales, CEMUPRO). Socialist Party of Santa Fe.

54. **July 2010. Lucas Sebastián Duran.** Member of the Radical Civic Union (Unión Cívica Radical).

ECUADOR

55. **13 November 2009. Osvaldo Hurtado.** Ex-President of Ecuador (1981–84). President of the Corporation for Developent Studies (Corporación de Estudios para el Desarrollo, Cordes).
56. **26 April 2010. Wilfredo Lucero.** Ex-President of the National Congress (2004–06). Deputy for the Democratic Left (Izquierda Democrática) (1996–98, 1988–92, 2003–07).
57. **26 April 2010. Rafael Dávila.** Assembly member for the Loja province for the Citizens' Conscience Movement (2009–13). Ex-Deputy for the Popular Democracy Party (1998–2000, 2003–05).
58. **26 April 2010. Paco Moncayo.** Ex-chief of the Joint Command of the Armed Forces of Ecuador (1995–98). Ex-mayor of the city of Quito (2001–05, 2005–08) for the Democratic Left Party. Assembly member for the province of Pichincha representing the Municipal Movement (2009–13).
59. **26 April 2010. Lucio Gutiérrez.** Ex-President of Ecuador (2003–05). Founding leader of the Patriotic Society Party.
60. **27 April 2010. Arturo Donoso.** Adviser to the governments of Osvaldo Hurtado, Rodrigo Borja and Sixto Durán.
61. **27 April 2010. Alberto Acosta.** President of the Constituent Assembly (2008). Ex-Minister of Energy (2007). Economic analyst. Professor/researcher at FLACSO Ecuador in Economics.
62. **27 April 2010. Betty Amores.** National Assembly member for Alianza PAIS (2009–13).
63. **28 April 2010. Francisco Ulloa.** Assembly member of the Democratic Popular Movement for the province of Cotopaxi (2009–13).
64. **28 April 2010. Fausto Cobo.** Deputy for the province of Pichincha for the Patriotic Society Party (2007).
65. **28 April 2010. Pedro Páez.** President of the board of the Central Bank of Ecuador. Ex-Minister and coordinator of economic policy (2007–09).
66. **28 April 2010. Jorge Escala.** National Assembly member for the MPD (2009–13).
67. **28 April 2010. Andrés Páez.** Assembly member for Pichincha for the Democratic Left (2009–13).
68. **29 April 2010. Pedro Saad.** Ex-communist leader.
69. **29 April 2010. Luis Fernando Torres.** Deputy for the province of Tungurahua for the Social Christian Party (2004–07).
70. **30 April 2010. Alexandra Vela.** Ex-National Deputy for the Popular Democracy Party (1998–2002).
71. **30 April 2010. Norman Wray.** Constituent Assembly member for the Breakaway 25 movement (Movimiento Ruptura de los 25) (2008). Councillor for the city of Quito (2009–13).
72. **30 April 2010. Virgilio Hernández.** Assembly member for the province of Pichincha for the Alianza PAIS (2009–13).

LIST OF INTERVIEWS 159

73. **3 May 2010. Alexandra Ocles.** National Secretary for the Social, Popular and Nationalities Movements of Ecuador in the government of Rafael Correa (2009–10). Member of the Breakaway 25 movement (Movimiento Ruptura de los 25).
74. **3 May 2010. Rodrigo Borja.** Ex-President of Ecuador (1988–92). Founder leader of the Democratic Left.
75. **3 May 2010. Sandra Alarcón.** Director of the Christian Democratic Union Party.
76. **5 May 2010. Dr César Montúfar.** Assembly member for Pichincha province representing the National Democratic Consensus Movement (2009–13).
77. **5 May 2010. Dr Rossana Alvarado.** Assembly member for the province of Azuay for Alianza PAIS (2009–13).
78. **18 May 2010. Dr María Paula Romo.** Assembly member for the province of Pichincha (2009–13). Member of the Breakaway 25 movement (Movimiento Ruptura de los 25).
79. **18 May 2010. Mariangel Muñoz.** Assembly member for the province of Azuay for Alianza PAIS (2009–13).
80. **25 May 2010. Linda Machuca.** Assembly member representing immigrants for Alianza PAIS (2009–13).
81. **26 May 2010. Silvia Salgado.** National Assembly member for the coalition between Alianza PAIS and the Ecuadorean Socialist Party (2009–13).
82. **26 May 2010. Marco Murillo.** Assembly member for the province of Chimborazo (2009–13). Member of the Amauta movement. Ex-leader of the FEINE. President of the Collective and Community Rights Commission of the National Assembly.
83. **2 June 2010. Fabricio Villamar.** Councillor for Quito for the National Democratic Consensus movement (2009–13).
84. **2 June 2010. Pedro de la Cruz.** National Assembly member for Alianza PAIS (2009–13).
85. **8 June 2010. Pablo Lucio-Paredes.** Constituent Assembly member for the Future Now movement (2008).
86. **15 June 2010. Ana María Larrea.** Under-Secretary of the Organization and Structure of the State of the National Secretariat of Planning and Development (Secretaría Nacional de Planificación y Desarrollo, SENPLADES).
87. **18 June 2010. Rafael Quintero.** Under-Secretary for multilateral affairs in the Ecuadorean chancellorship. Socialist leader.
88. **24 June 2010. Aminta Buenaño.** Assembly member for the province of Guayas for Alianza PAIS (2009–13).
89. **29 June 2010. Galo Lara.** Assembly member for the Los Ríos province for the Patriotic Society Party (2009–13).
90. **23 April 2010. Pablo Celi.** Director of the Sociology and Political Science School at the Central University of Ecuador.
91. **24 April 2010. Berta García.** Professor at the Pontificia Catholic University of Ecuador.
92. **26 April 2010. Jaime Arciniegas.** Union leader, ex-president of the Ecuadorean Confederation of Free Union Organizations (Confederación Ecuatoriana de Organizaciones Sindicales Libres, CEOSL) (2003–06).

93. **26 April 2010. Rocío Rosero.** Leader of the Ecuadorean feminist movement.
94. **27 April 2010. Ruth Hidalgo.** Sub-Director and legal adviser of the Citizen Participation Corporation.
95. **27 April 2010. Simón Jaramillo.** Citizen Participation Corporation.
96. **27 April 2010. Adrián Bonilla.** Director of FLACSO Ecuador.
97. **28 April 2010. Simón Pachano.** Coordinator of the Policy Studies Programme at FLACSO Ecuador.
98. **28 April 2010. Paco Rhon.** Director of the Andean Centre for Popular Action (Centro Andino de Acción Popular, CAAP).
99. **28 April 2010. Carlos de la Torre.** Professor/researcher at FLACSO Ecuador.
100. **29 April 2010. Diego Cano.** Head of the Federation of Petroleum Workers of Ecuador.
101. **29 April 2010. Franklin Ramírez.** Professor/researcher at FLACSO Ecuador.
102. **29 April 2010. Fernando Villavicencio.** Ex-petroleum workers' leader, political activist, member of the Democratic Pole Movement (Movimiento Polo Democrático).
103. **17 May 2010. Ricardo Ulcuango.** Indigenous leader, ex-deputy of the Pichincha province for the Pachacutik movement (2003–07). Ex-Vice-President of the Confederation of Ecuadorean Indigenous Nationalities (Confederación de nacionalidades indígenas ecuatorianas, CONAIE).
104. **31 May 2010. Delfín Tenesaca.** President of the indigenous organization ECUARUNARI.
105. **7 June 2010. Marlon Santí.** President of the Confederation of Ecuadorean Indigenous Nationalities (Confederación de nacionalidades indígenas ecuatorianas, CONAIE).
106. **7 June 2010. Luis Andrango.** President of the National Federation of Peasant, Indigenous and Black Organizations of Ecuador (Federación nacional de organizaciones campesinas, indígenas y negras del Ecuador, FENOCIN).
107. **3 May 2010. Ernesto Aranibar.** Director of the Democracy Now Corporation (Ágora Democrática, IDEA).
108. **4 May 2010. Sandy Quimbaya.** Coordinator of the NDI headquarters.
109. **13 May 2010. Jimmy Bejarano.** Director of the school of leadership of the National Democratic Consensus movement.
110. **28 May 2010. Patricio Coba.** Director of the 'Manuel Córdova Galarza' Institute of Policy Formation, an institute of the Democratic Left party.
111. **1 June 2010. Raúl Proaño.** Director of the school of citizenship of the Truirbas collective.
112. **8 June 2010. Dolores Padilla.** Coordinator of Leadership Projects at the Esquel Foundation.
113. **9 June 2010. Carla Bonilla.** Coordinator of Leadership Projects at the Konrad Adenauer Foundation.
114. **18 June 2010. Juan Pablo Espinoza.** Director of the school of leadership of Movimiento Ruptura de los 25.
115. **22 June 2010. Norma Mayo.** Director of the CONAIE school of leadership for indigenous women.

116. **23 June 2010. Stalin Vargas.** Director of the Popular Democratic Movement school of policy training.
117. **1 July 2010. Adriana Egas Aráuz.** Christian Democratic Union, Christian Democratic Youth.
118. **1 July 2010. Andrés de la Vega Grunauer.** Member of Alianza PAIS.

VENEZUELA

119. **3 October 2011. Ramón Guillermo Aveledo.** Executive Secretary of the Mesa de Unidad Democrática (MUD).
120. **4 October 2011. Biagio Pileri.** Deputy of the MUD representing the state of Yaracuy.
121. **5 October 2011. Fausto Maso.** Journalist, speaker, political analyst.
122. **5 October 2011. Freddy Guevara.** Councillor for the metropolitan area of Caracas (2008–12) and President of the Citizens' Security Commission and DDHH of the city.
123. **5 October 2011. Stalin González.** Deputy for Caracas in the National Assembly for the Nuevo Tiempo party.
124. **5 October 2011. María Corina Machado.** Deputy for Miranda state (2011–15).
125. **5 October 2011. Ramón José Medina.** Coordinator of International Affairs at the MUD.
126. **6 October 2011. Teodoro Petkoff.** Venezuelan politician, journalist and economist.
127. **6 October 2011. Pedro Benítez.** Coordinator of the MUD.
128. **6 October 2011. Héctor Constant.** Bureaucrat at the Ministry of Foreign Affairs in the 'Pedro Gual' Institute of High Diplomatic Studies.
129. **6 October 2011. Carlos Ocariz.** Mayor of the Sucre municipality for Justice First (Primero Justicia).
130. **7 October 2011. Guillermo Miguelena.** Secretary for International Affairs at the Youth Bureau of Democratic Action (Acción Democrática).
131. **5 October 2011. Luis Velásquez.** Deputy for the Caracas metropolitan area for the Partido Voluntad Popular.
132. **7 October 2011. Alejandro Vivas.** Deputy for the Caracas metropolitan area. COPEI party.
133. **7 October 2011. Juan Guaido.** Deputy in the National Assembly for the state of Vargas. Partido Voluntad Popular.
134. **14 October 2011. Tomas Guanipa.** Secretary General of the Partido Primero Justicia. Deputy in the National Assembly for the state of Zulia.
135. **29 November 2011. Rodolfo Rodríguez.** Deputy in the National Assembly for Anzoategui. AD party.
136. **21 December 2011. Angel Medina.** Deputy in the National Assembly for Miranda. AD party.
137. **21 December 2011. Edgar Zambrano.** Deputy in the National Assembly for the state of Lara. AD party.
138. **3 October 2011. Feliciano Reyna.** President of Solidarity Action (Acción Solidaria).

139. **3 October 2011. Carlos Correa.** Director of Public Space – area of human rights.
140. **3 October 2011. Luis Vicente León.** President of Datanalisis.
141. **4 October 2011. Alfredo Padilla.** Union member and member of the International Workers Organization.
142. **4 October 2011. Albis Muñoz.** Ex-President of Fedecamaras.
143. **4 October 2011. Deborah Van Berkel.** Vice-President, Venezuelan Institute of Social and Political Studies (Instituto Venezolano de Estudios Sociales y Políticos, INVESP).
144. **4 October 2011. Alejandro Oropeza.** Director of Projects – Legal Consultant at the Hannah Arendt Observatory.
145. **4 October 2011. Heinz Sonntag.** Director General of the Hannah Arendt Observatory.
146. **5 October 2011. Georg Eickhoff.** Director of the Konrad Adenauer Foundation (KAS).
147. **5 October 2011. Marino Alvarado Betancourt.** Director of the Venezuelan Programme for Education and Action on Human Rights (Programa Venezolano de Educación-Acción en Derechos Humanos, PROVEA).
148. **6 October 2011. José Manuel González de Tober.** Ex-business leader at Fedecamaras.
149. **6 October 2011. Diana Vegas Castro.** Director of the Centre for Service of Popular Action (CESAP).
150. **7 October 2011. Aldo de Santis.** Coordinator of the Centre of Public Policy (IFEDEC).
151. **22 October 2011. Miguel Sabal.** Director of the Present Future Foundation.
152. **17 December 2011. Isabel Carmona.** Democratic Action Training School.
153. **18 December 2011. Benigno Alarcón.** Director of the school of social and community leaders at the Andrés Bello Catholic University (Universidad Católica Andrés Bello, UCAB).
154. **3 October 2011. Germán Carrera.** Doctor of History.
155. **5 October 2011. Francine Jacome.** Director of the Venezuelan Institute of Social and Political Studies (Instituto Venezolano de Estudios Sociales y Políticos, INVESP) and Regional Director of Research at the Regional Network of Economic and Social Research (Coordinadora Regional de Investigaciones Económicas y Sociales, CRIES).
156. **6 October 2011. John Magdaleno.** Political scientist at USB. Specialist in social science data analysis at the Central University of Venezuela (Universidad Central de Venezuela, UCV).
157. **6 October 2011. Carlos Luna Ramírez.** Teaching adviser at the Delegation of the School of Political and Administrative Studies at the Central University of Venezuela.
158. **7 October 2011. María Teresa Romero.** Professor at the UCV.
159. **7 October 2011. Carlos Romero.** Professor at the UCV.
160. **7 October 2011. Nicmer Evans.** Teacher at the School of Sociology at the UCV.
161. **5 October 2011. Marisela Boada.** Leader of the PSUV, Metropolitan Deputy.

162. **5 October 2011. Luis Velasquez.** Deputy for the metropolitan area of Caracas. Partido Voluntad Popular.
163. **7 October 2011. Alejandro Vivas.** Deputy for the metropolitan area of Caracas. COPEI party.
164. **7 October 2011. Juan Guaido.** Deputy in the National Assembly. Partido Voluntad Popular.
165. **14 October 2011. Tomas Guanipa.** Secretary General, Partido Primero Justicia.
166. **4 November 2011. Alfonzo Marquina.** Deputy in the National Assembly for Miranda. UNT party.
167. **4 November 2011. Juan Carlos Caldera.** Deputy in the National Assembly for Miranda. Partido Primero Justicia.
168. **29 November 2011. Rodolfo Rodríguez.** Deputy in the National Assembly for Anzoategui. Democratic Action Party.
169. **21 December 2011. Ángel Medina.** Deputy in the National Assembly for Miranda. Democratic Action Party.
170. **21 December 2011. Edgar Zambrano.** Deputy in the National Assembly for the state of Lara. Democratic Action Party.
171. **5 October 2011. Ángel Lugo.** Political Secretary of Democratic Action.
172. **22 October 2011. Miguel Sabal.** Director of the Present Future Foundation.
173. **17 December 2011. Isabel Carmona.** Democratic Action Training School.
174. **1 July 2010. Juan Pablo López Gross.** Member of the Voluntad Popular party.
175. **1 July 2010. María Francia Herrera.** Member of Partido Primero Justicia.

COLOMBIA

176. **10 October 2011. Rafael Pardo.** Leader of the Liberal Party (2010). Senator of the Republic (2002–06). Professor and researcher, University of los Andes.
177. **10 October 2011. Jorge Robledo.** Senator of the Alternative Democratic Pole (Polo Democrático Alternativo) (2010–14).
178. **10 October 2011. José Darío Salazar.** President of the National Conservative Directorate.
179. **10 October 2011. Camilo González Posso.** Director of the Institute of Development for Peace (Instituto de Desarrollo para la Paz, INDEPAZ).
180. **10 October 2011. Salud Hernández Mora.** Journalist on *El Tiempo*.
181. **11 October 2011. Armando Benedetti.** Senator of the U party (2010–14).
182. **11 October 2011. Carlos Amaya.** Representative of the Green Party.
183. **11 October 2011. Roy Barreras.** Senator of the U party (2010–14).
184. **11 October 2011. Angelino Garzón.** Vice-President of the nation in the presidency of Juan Manuel Santos Calderón.
185. **12 October 2011. Mauricio Ernesto Ospina Gómez.** Senator of the Polo Democrático Alternativo (2010–14).
186. **12 October 2011. Iván Cepeda.** Representative of the Polo Democrático Alternativo (2010–14).
187. **12 October 2011. David Luna.** Member of the Chamber of Representatives of Colombia.

188. **12 October 2011. Germán Navas Talero.** Representative in the Chamber for the Polo Democrático Alternativo (2010–14).
189. **12 October 2011. Marta Lucia Ramírez.** Ex-Minister of Defence (2002–03).
190. **13 October 2011. Clara López Obregón.** Mayor of Bogotá (2011).
191. **13 October 2011. Wilson Arias.** Representative in the Chamber for the Polo Democrático Alternativo.
192. **13 October 2011. Germán Varón.** Representative in the Chamber for Cambio Radical (2010–14).
193. **13 October 2011. Dr Alberto Echavarría.** Vice-President for Judicial and Social Affairs of the National Association of Entrepreneurs of Colombia (Asuntos Jurídicos y Sociales de la Asociación Nacional de Empresarios de Colombia, ANDI).
194. **13 October 2011. Gloria Inés Ramírez Ríos.** Senator of the Polo Democrático Alternativo (2010–14).
195. **13 October 2011. Horacio José Serpa.** Councillor elect for Bogotá for the Liberal Party (2012–15).
196. **13 October 2011. John Sudarsky.** Senator of the Green Party (2010–14).
197. **13 October 2011. Jonathan Forero.** Adviser to the head of the Bogotá Council. Youth President of the U party.
198. **14 October 2011. Gustavo Gallón.** Colombian Commission of Lawyers (1988–2011).
199. **14 October 2011. Luis Eduardo Celís.** Coordinator of the public policy for peace, Corporación Nuevo Arco Iris.
200. **14 October 2011. Lázaro Ramírez.** President of the Colombian Union of Young Democrats (Unión Colombiana de Jóvenes Demócratas, UCJD).
201. **11 October 2011. Pedro Santana.** President of Long Live the Citizenry.
202. **12 October 2011. Olga Lucía Gómez.** Director of the Free Country Foundation.
203. **14 October 2011. Mauricio Romero Vidal.** Director of the Observatory of Armed Conflict, Corporación Nuevo Arco Iris (2008–11).
204. **10 October 2011. María Victoria Llorente.** Principal Researcher for the Group and Executive Director of the Foundation for Ideas for Peace (Fundación Ideas para la Paz, FIP).
205. **11 October 2011. Alejo Vargas Velásquez.** Professor, National University, and Director of the Research Group on Security and Defence.
206. **12 October 2011. Alexandra Barrios.** Director of the Electoral Observer Mission (Misión de Observación Electoral, MOE).
207. **12 October 2011. Francisco Leal Buitrago.** Honorary professor at the National and Los Andes universities.
208. **12 October 2011. Oscar Fernando Sevillano.** Assistant researcher, Observatory of Armed Conflict of the Corporación Nuevo Arco Iris (2006–).
209. **14 October 2011. Fernán González.** Researcher at CINEP and ex-director of the institute.
210. **9 February 2012. Ángela Robledo.** Representative in the Chamber for the Green Party.
211. **21 February 2012. Maritza Martínez.** Senator, U party (2010–14).
212. **9 March 2012. Gilma Jiménez.** Senator, Green Party.

213. **21 March 2012. Marco Aníbal Avirama.** Senator, Independent Social Alliance Party (Partido Alianza Social Independiente, ASI).
214. **28 March 2012. Germán Carlosama.** Senator, Colombian Indigenous Authorities Party (Partido Autoridades Indígenas de Colombia, AICO).
215. **29 March 2012. Rodrigo Villalba.** Senator, Colombian Liberal Party.
216. **8 May 2012. Édgar Espíndola.** Senator, National Integration Party (Partido de Integración Nacional, PIN).
217. **8 May 2012. Antonio Correa.** Senator, National Integration Party (Partido de Integración Nacional, PIN).
218. **8 May 2012. Juan Carlos Salazar.** Representative in the Chamber of the National Integration Party (Partido de Integración Nacional, PIN).
219. **9 May 2012. Eduardo Carlos Merlano.** Senator, U party.
220. **1 March 2012. Carolina Montoya.** School of Government, MIRA movement.
221. **12 March 2012. Paola Andrea Pinilla.** Hernán Echavarría Olozága Political Science Institute (Instituto de Ciencia Política, ICP).
222. **14 March 2012. Miguel Galvis.** 'People's' School of policy formation, Independent Social Alliance Party (Partido Alianza Social Independiente, ASI).
223. **15 March 2012. Álvaro Forero.** Leadership and Democracy Foundation, young politicians' training programme.
224. **28 March 2012. Dr Arnobio Cordoba.** Director, Phelps Stokes Foundation – Colombia.
225. **17 April 2012. Alfonso Amaya Parra.** Alberto Lleras Camargo School of Government, Los Andes University.
226. **23 April 2012. Carlos Martínez.** Centre for Conservative Party Thought.
227. **25 April 2012. Hugo Guerra.** Liberal Thought Institute (Instituto de Pensamiento Liberal, IPL).
228. **4 May 2012. Catalina Nava.** Youth member of the Polo Democrático Alternativo.
229. **1 July 2010. Jessica Pamela Obando Burgos.** Colombian Liberal Party.

URUGUAY

230. **21 March 2011. Dr Julio Ma. Sanguinetti.** Senator of the Republic (2005–10) and Constitutional President of Uruguay (1985–90, 1995–2000).
231. **21 March 2011. Fitzgerald Cantero Piali.** National Deputy for Montevideo for the Colorado Party (2010–15).
232. **22 March 2011. Jorge Saravia.** Senator of the Republic for Frente Amplio.
233. **22 March 2011. Pablo Mieres.** Leader of the Independent Party.
234. **22 March 2011. Alfonso P. Varela.** President of the National Chamber of Commerce and Services of Uruguay.
235. **23 March 2011. Heber da Rosa.** Senator of the Republic, National Alliance, National Party (2010–15).
236. **23 March 2011. Rafael Michelini.** Senator of the Republic for Frente Amplio – Liber Seregni Front (2010–15).
237. **23 March 2011. Carlos Julio Pereyra.** Ex-President of the Board of the National Party (2008–09).
238. **23 March 2011. Raúl Sendic.** President of ANCAP (petroleum, gas and alcohol refinery).

239. **23 March 2011. Francisco Gallinal.** Senator of the Republic, National Unity, National Party (2010–15).
240. **23 March 2011. Alberto Couriel.** Senator of the Republic, Frente Amplio – Space 609 (2010–15).
241. **23 March 2011. Luis Rosadilla.** Minister of Defence (2010–). Deputy of the Popular Participation Movement (Movimiento de Participación Popular, MPP) (2005–09).
242. **23 March 2011. Dr Luis Alberto Lacalle.** Senator of the Republic, National Party (2010–15).
243. **24 March 2011. Danilo Astori.** Vice-President of the Republic (2010–11).
244. **25 March 2011. Felipe Michelini.** National Deputy, Frente Amplio (2010–15).
245. **25 March 2011. Juan Castillo.** Coordinator of the Secretariat of International affairs – PIT CNT (trade union workers' plenary).
246. **11 April 2011. Lucía Topolansky.** Senator of the Republic, Frente Amplio – Space 609/MPP (2010–15).
247. **11 April 2011. Carlos Moreira.** Senator of the Republic, National Alliance, National Party (2010–15).
248. **11 April 2011. José Bayardi.** National Deputy for Montevideo, Frente Amplio. Minister of Defence (2008–09).
249. **12 April 2011. Jorge Luis Batlle Ibáñez.** Ex-President of Uruguay (2000–05), Colorado Party.
250. **12 April 2011. Alberto Casas.** National Deputy for the Department of San José, National Party (2010–15).
251. **12 April 2011. Carmelo Vidalín.** National Deputy for the Department of Durazno, National Party (2010–15).
252. **12 April 2011. Jorge Chediak.** Minister of the Supreme Court of Justice (2009–).
253. **12 April 2011. Ricardo Berois.** National Deputy for the Department of Flores, National Party (2010–15).
254. **13 April 2011. Álvaro Delgado.** National Deputy, National Party, National Unity (2010–15).
255. **13 April 2011. Amin Niffouri.** National Deputy for the Department of Canelones, List 400, National Party (2010–15).
256. **14 April 2011. Jorge Gandini.** National Deputy for Montevideo, National Party (2010–15).
257. **14 April 2011. Nelson Mancedo.** Secretary of Finance of the Broad Front. Member of the Uruguayan Communist Party.
258. **14 April 2011. Verónica Alonso.** National Deputy for Montevideo, National Party (2010–15).
259. **14 April 2011. Constanza Moreira.** Senator of the Republic, Frente Amplio, Space 609 (2010–15).
260. **14 April 2011. Eduardo Fernández.** Secretary General of the Socialist Party (2006–).
261. **26 April 2011. Graciela Matiaude.** National Deputy for the Department of Canelones, Colorado Party, Let's Go Uruguay (2010–15).

262. **27 April 2011. Dr Alfredo Solari.** Senator of the Republic, Colorado Party, Let's Go Uruguay (2010–15).
263. **28 April 2011. Gustavo Penadés.** Senator of the Republic, National Party, National Unity (2010–15).
264. **29 April 2011. Pedro Saravia.** National Deputy for the Department of Cerro Largo, National Party (2010–15).
265. **9 May 2011. Martín Tierno.** National Deputy for the Department of Durazno, Frente Amplio, Space 609 (2010–15).
266. **9 May 2011. Andrés Lima.** National Deputy for the Department of Salto, Frente Amplio (2010–15).
267. **11 May 2011. Daniel Bianchi.** National Deputy for the Department of Colonia, Colorado Party, Let's Go Uruguay (2010–15).
268. **16 May 2011. Gustavo Cersósimo.** National Deputy for the Department of San José, Colorado Party, Let's Go Uruguay (2010–15).
269. **19 May 2011. Sebastián Sabini.** National Deputy for the Department of Canelones, Frente Amplio, Space 609 (2010–15).
270. **21 March 2011. Romeo Pérez.** Political scientist, President of the Council of the Latin American Human Economy Centre (Centro Latinoamericano de Economía Humana, CLAEH) (2010–13).
271. **22 March 2011. Eduardo Bottinelli.** Director of the FACTUM consultancy.
272. **12 April 2011. Juan Gabito Zóboli.** Director of the 'Manuel Oribe' Institute.
273. **13 April 2011. Adolfo Pérez Piera.** Ex President of the Council for Transparency and Public Ethics (Junta de Transparencia y Ética Pública, JUTEP).
274. **14 April 2011. Luis E. González.** Director and co-founder of CIFRA.
275. **14 April 2011. Agustín Canzani.** Director of the Líber Seregni Foundation.
276. **25 April 2011. Milton Castellano.** Director of the Cuesta Duarte Institute.
277. **25 April 2011. Gonzalo Kmaid.** Director of Projects and Senior Researcher at CIFRA.
278. **21 March 2011. Daniel Buquet.** Academic at the Institute of Political Science, Faculty of Social Sciences, University of the Republic.
279. **24 March 2011. Adolfo Garcé.** Academic, Political Science Institute, Faculty of Social Sciences (UDELAR).
280. **12 May 2011. Miguel Serna.** Academic. Researcher and professor in the Sociology Department at the Faculty of Social Sciences, University of the Republic.
281. **13 May 2011. Jorge Lanzaro.** Academic. Researcher at the Political Science Institute, University of the Republic.
282. **13 May 2011. Dr José Rilla.** Academic. Professor at the Faculty of Social Sciences, University of the Republic.
283. **14 May 2011. Gustavo Adrián de Armas.** Academic. Sociologist, Faculty of Social Sciences, University of the Republic.
284. **15 May 2011. Hebert Gatto.** Ex-Professor of Political Science at the University of the Republic.
285. **1 July 2010. Damián Payotti de León.** Frente Amplio. University of the Republic.

WASHINGTON, DC

286. **5 March 2012. Miriam Harmer.** Legislative adviser. Specialist in foreign relations for Republican Senator Mike Lee (Utah).

287. **5 March 2012. Joan Caivano.** Assistant to the President and Director of Special Projects at the Inter-American Dialogue.

288. **6 March 2012. Dan Fisk.** Republican International Institute.

289. **6 March 2012. Jorge Arguello.** Ambassador of the Argentine Republic to the United States.

290. **6 March 2012. Daniel Erikson.** Senior Adviser on Western Hemisphere Affairs at the US Department of State.

291. **6 March 2012. Michael Shifter.** President of the Inter-American Dialogue.

292. **6 March 2012. José Miguel Vivanco.** Director, Division of the Americas, Human Rights Watch.

293. **7 March 2012. Miriam Kornblith.** Regional Director of the Latin America and Caribbean Programme, National Endowment for Democracy.

294. **7 March 2012. Heather Booth.** President of the MidWest Academy.

295. **7 March 2012. Augusta Babson.** Official in public diplomacy at the US Department of State, Office of the Principal Adviser to the Secretary for Civil Society and Emerging Democracies.

296. **7 March 2012. Robert Creamer.** Political and strategy consultant.

297. **8 March 2012. José Miguel Insulza.** Secretary General of the Organization of American States (OAS).

298. **8 March 2012. Melanie Sloan.** Executive Director of Citizens for Responsibility and Ethics in Washington (CREW).

299. **8 March 2012. Jim Swigert.** Senior Associate and Regional Director for Latin America and the Caribbean at the National Democratic Institute (NDI) for international affairs.

300. **8 March 2012. Theodore Piccone.** Senior Fellow and Deputy Director, Foreign Policy at the Brookings Institution.

301. **9 March 2012. Sam Farr.** US representative for California's 17th congressional district, serving since 1993. Member of the Democratic Party.

302. **9 March 2012. Nina M. Serafino.** Expert in international security, foreign affairs, defence, Commercial Service Division of the research service at the Library of Congress.

303. **9 March 2012. Enrique Fernandez Toledo.** Deputy Chief of Staff of the Democratic Representative for Illinois, Luis Gutiérrez.

304. **9 March 2012. Tina Huang.** Foreign affairs officer, Bureau of Western Hemisphere Affairs, State Department.

305. **9 March 2012. Francisco Javier González.** Director of the Bureau of Western Hemisphere Affairs, State Department.

306. **5 March 2012. Mark Sullivan.** Specialist in international security, Congressional Research Service on Foreign Relations, Defence and Trade.

307. **6 March 2012. Arturo Valenzuela.** Professor of Government and Director of the Centre for Latin American Studies at Georgetown University. United

States Assistant Secretary of State for Western Hemisphere Affairs, nominated by President Barack Obama.

308. **7 March 2012. Christopher Arterton.** Academic. Professor of Political Management at the George Washington University Graduate School of Political Management (GSPM).

309. **7 March 2012. Luis Matos.** Professor at George Washington University.

310. **8 March 2012. James Thurber.** Professor and Director of the Centre for Congressional and Presidential Studies.

311. **7 March 2012. Mark Feierstein.** Associate administrator of USAID for Latin America and the Caribbean.

312. **6 March 2012. Silvio Waisbord.** Associate professor and Director of the Graduate Programme at the School of Media and Public Affairs at George Washington University.

NEW YORK

313. **28 February 2012. Jimmy Tom.** Director of the NY Centre Foundation, NY Library.

314. **29 February 2012. Kenneth Erickson.** Graduate Centre, City University of New York (CUNY).

315. **1 March 2012. Heraldo Muñoz.** Under-Secretary General of the UN Development Programme (UNDP) (May 2010). Regional Director of the UNDP for Latin America and the Caribbean.

316. **1 March 2012. Gerardo Noto.** Specialist on the Democratic governability programme, Regional Board for Latin America and the Caribbean.

317. **1 March 2012. Roland Rich.** Chief Executive of the UN Democracy Fund (UNDEF). Official in charge, United Nations Office for Project Services (UNOP).

318. **2 March 2012. Victoria Murillo.** Professor of Political Science and International Relations at the Universities of Columbia and Yale.

319. **2 March 2012. Susan L. Woodward.** Professor in the Political Science Programme at the Centre for Graduate Studies, City University of New York (CUNY).

Notes

INTRODUCTION

1. In order to avoid 'he/she' we have decided to use 'he' as our default pronoun.

CHAPTER 1

1. Our research project included trips to Washington, DC, and New York to discuss our main ideas with academics and consultants. The total number of interviewees is 319. However, only 285 of them were political leaders in Bogotá, Buenos Aires, Caracas, Montevideo and Quito.
2. In this book we refer only to interviews conducted with politicians, legislators and party leaders. We do not include interviews with academics and journalists.
3. The interviews were conducted between 2009 and 2013. It is well known that the use of this new technology, especially Twitter, has become more important over the last two years.

CHAPTER 2

1. This list includes Hernán Siles Zuazo (Bolivia, 1985), Raúl Alfonsín (Argentina, 1989), Fernando Collor de Mello (Brazil, 1992), Jorge Serrano (Guatemala, 1993), Carlos Andrés Pérez (Venezuela, 1993), Jean-Bertrand Aristide (Haití, 1994 and 2004), Joaquín Balaguer (Dominican Republic, 1996), Abdalá Bucaram (Ecuador, 1997), Raúl Cubas (Paraguay, 1999), Jamil Mahuad (Ecuador, 2000), Alberto Fujimori (Peru, 2000), Valentín Paniagua (Peru, 2001), Fernando de la Rúa (Argentina, 2001), Alberto Rodríguez Saá (Argentina, 2001), Ramón Puerta (Argentina, 2002), Gonzalo Sánchez de Lozada (Bolivia, 2003), Eduardo Duhalde (Argentina, 2003), Lucio Gutiérrez (Ecuador, 2005), Carlos Mesa (Bolivia, 2005), Manuel Zelaya (Honduras, 2009) and Fernando Lugo (Paraguay, 2012).

CHAPTER 3

1. The 2011 UNDP Report on Human Development in Colombia states that 52 per cent of property is held by just 1.15 per cent of the population (La Vanguardia 2011).
2. The period of '*La Violencia*' lasted from 1948 to 1957, especially under the dictatorship of Gustavo Rojas Pinilla (1953–57). Terrible atrocities were committed during that time. For example, the head of the Liberal Party, Jorge Eliécer Gaitán, was assassinated on 9 April 1948 in a street uprising known as the *Bogotazo*. Over 200,000 civilians were killed (Morales 1978: 59).
3. The scandal of false positives was reported in 2008 and involved members of the Colombian army. The soldiers killed innocent civilians and then made out that they were dead guerrillas. These murders were presented as successes in the fight against the FARC. These extrajudicial executions were denounced nationally and internationally by Philip Alston, special reporter to the UN for arbitrary executions, in May 2010.

CHAPTER 4

1. In Argentina fifty-four interviews were conducted between December 2009 and August 2010 and in Ecuador sixty-four interviews were conducted between April and August 2010.
2. After resignations and deaths, the Court now has five members.
3. Raúl Alfonsín issued ten, Carlos Menem 545, Fernando de la Rúa 74, Eduardo Duhalde 160 and Néstor Kirchner between 236 and 270 (Carrera 2013). Cristina Fernández had issued thirty-two NUDs up to December 2014.
4. La Cámpora takes its name from Héctor J. Cámpora, a loyal follower of Juan Péron. Cámpora was president in 1973. He prepared the way for Perón to return to the Casa Rosada.
5. Our respondents mentioned Juan José Flores (the first president, who served for three periods: 1830–34, 1839–43 and 1843–45), Gabriel García Moreno (president 1859–65 and 1869–75), José Eloy Alfaro (president 1897 and 1901 and 1906–11), José María Velasco Ibarra (president for five periods: 1934–35, 1944–47, 1952–56, 1960–61 and 1968–72), León Febres Cordero (president 1984 and 1988) and Rafael Correa (president from 2007).
6. Ecuadorean constitutional history has been volatile. From 1830 to the present there have been twenty Constitutions; the last was approved under the Correa government in 2008. All the interviewees praised the current Constitution and it is definitely a progressive, modern, broad legal framework which includes social rights such as the right to live well, the right of people and groups to priority attention, legal instruments on biodiversity and natural resources and rules of organization for political parties.
7. One of our interviewees stated that, for example, 90 per cent of the rural inhabitants of Cotopaxi receive the *Bono*.
8. This refers to the weekly radio programme that Rafael Correa broadcasts on Saturday mornings.

Bibliography

Abente Brun, D. and L. Diamond (eds) (2014) *Clientelism, Social Policy and the Quality of Democracy*, Baltimore, MD: Johns Hopkins University Press.

Alcántara, M. (2004) ¿*Instituciones o máquinas ideológicas? Origen, programa y organización de los partidos latinoamericanos*, Barcelona: Universidad Autónoma de Barcelona.

Arditi, B. (2004) 'El populismo como espectro de la democracia: una respuesta a Canovan', *Political Studies*, 52(1): 135–43.

Arnson, C., J. Jara and C. Escobar (2009) 'Pobreza, desigualdad y la nueva izquierda en América Latina', *Woodrow Wilson Center Update on the Americas*, 6, October.

Auyero, J. (2004) *Clientelismo político. Las caras ocultas*, Buenos Aires: Capital Intelectual, Colección Claves para Todos.

Azorín, F. and J. L. Sánchez-Crespo (1986) *Métodos y Aplicaciones del Muestreo*, Madrid: Alianza Editorial.

Barreda, M. (2011) 'La calidad de la democracia: un análisis comparado de América Latina', *Política y gobierno*, XVIII(2).

Batlle, M. and J. R. Puyana (2011) 'El nivel de nacionalización del sistema de partidos colombiano: una mirada a partir de las elecciones legislativas de 2010', *Colombia Internacional*, 74: 27–57.

Bittner, A. (2011) *Platform or Personality? The Role of Party Leaders in Elections*, Oxford: Oxford University Press.

Blondel, J. (1987) *Political Leadership*, London: Sage.

Boin, A., P. 't Hart and F. van Esch (2012) 'Political leadership in times of crisis: comparing leader responses to financial turbulence', in L. Helms, *Comparative Political Leadership*, Basingstoke: Palgrave Macmillan.

Bonilla González, R. (2011) 'Apertura y reprimarización de la economía colombiana. Un paraíso de corto plazo', *Nueva Sociedad*, vol. 231, 46–65.

Botana, N. (2006) *Poder y hegemonía*, Buenos Aires: Emecé.

Botinelli, E. (2008) 'Las carreras políticas de los senadores en Uruguay: ¿cambios o continuidades ante el triunfo de la izquierda?', *Revista de Sociología e Política*, 16(30): 29–43.

Brown, A. (2014) *The Myth of the Strong Leader. Political Leadership in the Modern Age*, London: Bodley Head.

Bueno de Mesquita, B. and A. Smith (2011) *The Dictator's Handbook. Why bad behavior is almost always good politics*, Philadelphia, PA: PublicAffairs.

Buquet, D. (2000) 'La elección uruguaya después de la reforma electoral de 1997: los cambios que aseguraron la continuidad', *Perfiles Latinoamericanos*, 16.

—— (2014) 'Estudio sobre la imagen pública del poder legislativo', Convenio Poder Legislativo, Instituto de Ciencia Política, 47ª Legislatura, March, www.comunicacion2000.com/rnu-audio/uruguay/1408/Informe%203%20%20Imagen%20P%FAblica%20PL%202013.pdf.

Buquet, D. and D. Chasquetti (2005) 'Elecciones en Uruguay 2004: descifrando el cambio', *Revista Uruguaya de Ciencia Política*, 25(2): 143–52.

Burns, J. (1978) *Leadership*, New York: Harper Perennial.

Calvo, E. and M. V. Murillo (forthcoming) 'Selecting clients: partisan networks and the electoral benefits of targeted distribution'.

Cannon, B. (2009) *Hugo Chávez and the Bolivarian Revolution: Populism and Democracy in a Globalised Age*, Manchester: Manchester University Press.

Cárdenas Ruiz, J. D. (2012) 'Una aproximación a la cultura política colombiana desde el debate contemporáneo de la democracia', *Revista Facultad de Derecho y Ciencias Políticas*, 42(117): 393–424.

Cardoso, F. H. (2006) 'El populismo amenaza con regresar a América Latina', *Clarín*, 18 June.

Carrera, A. (2013) Argentina: Decretos de Necesidad y Urgencia en el período 2007–2011, *Revista de Ciencia Política de La Ciudad de Buenos Aires* (19) http://www.revcienciapolitica.com.ar/num19art4.php

Cason, J. (2002) 'Electoral reform, institutional change and party adaptation in Uruguay', *Latin American Politics and Society*, 44(3): 89–109.

CEPAL (2012) *Panorama Social 2012*, Santiago: CEPAL.

Chhokar, J., F. Brodbeck and R. House (eds) (2007) *Culture and Leadership across the World. The GLOBE Book of In-Depth Studies of 25 Societies*, New Jersey: LEA.

Choi, S. (2007) 'Democratic leadership: the lessons of exemplary models for democratic governance', *International Journal of Leadership Studies*, 2(3): 243–62.

Clarín (2011) www.clarin.com/politica/Presupuesto-volvera-Gobierno-dibujar-cuentas_0_547745347.html.

Cleary, M. (2008) 'Explaining the left's resurgence', in L. Diamond, M. Plattner and D. Abente Brun, *Latin America's Struggle for Democracy*, Baltimore, MD: Johns Hopkins University Press.

Conaghan, C. and C. de la Torre (2008) 'The permanent campaign of Rafael Correa: making Ecuador's plebiscitary presidency', *International Journal of Press/Politics*, 13(3): 267–84.

Coppedge, M. (1998) 'The dynamic diversity of Latin American party systems', *Party Politics*, 4(4): 547–68.

Corral, F. (2010) 'Caudillos, crédulos y cortesanos', *Polemika, Revista Cuatrimestral del Instituto de Economía*, 1(3): 30–42.

Corrales, J. (2002) 'The politics of Argentina's meltdown', *World Policy Journal*, 19(3): 29–42.

—— (2010) 'The repeating revolution: Chavez's new politics and old economics', in K. Weyland, R. Madrid and W. Hunter (eds), *Leftist Governments in Latin America: Successes and Shortcomings*, New York: Cambridge University Press.

Corrales, J. and M. Penfold (2007) 'Venezuela: crowding out the opposition', *Journal of Democracy*, 18(2): 99–113.

Crisp, B. (1997) *El control institucional de la participación en Venezuela*, Caracas: Editorial Jurídica Venezolana.

Dahl, R. (1961) *Who Governs? Democracy and power in an American city*, New Haven, CT: Yale University Press.

Danza, A. and E. Tulbovitz (2015) *Una oveja negra al poder*, Buenos Aires: Sudamericana.

Darcy de Oliveira, M. (2008) 'Deepening democracy in Latin America', in M. Albrow et al., *Global Civil Society 2007/2008, Communicative Power and Democracy*, London: Sage.

Dávila Ladrón de Guevara, A. (1997) 'Democracia pactada. El Frente Nacional y el proyecto constituyente del 91 en Colombia', PhD thesis, FLACSO, Mexico, www .flacso.edu.mx/biblioiberoamericana/TEXT/DOCCS_I_promocion_1995-1997/ Davila_ARES.pdf, pp. 155–8.

De Armas, G. (2010) 'Debilitamiento del efecto demográfico y consolidación de un nuevo sistema de partidos: evidencia de las elecciones 2009 en Uruguay', *Revista Uruguaya de Ciencia Política*, 18(1): 41–63.

De la Torre, C. (2008) 'Populismo, ciudadanía y Estado de derecho', in C. de la Torre and E. Peruzzotti, *El retorno del pueblo. Populismo y nuevas democracias en América Latina*, Quito: FLACSO/Ecuador and Ministry of Culture.

—— (2013a) 'El liderazgo populista de Rafael Correa y la desinstitucionalización de la política', in R. Diamint and L. Tedesco (eds), *Democratizar a los políticos. Un estudio sobre líderes latinoamericanos*, Madrid: Libros de la Catarata.

—— (2013b) 'El tecnopopulismo de Rafael Correa', *Latin American Research Review*, 48(1): 24–43.

De la Torre, C. and C. Conaghan (2009) 'The hybrid campaign: tradition and modernity in Ecuador's 2006 presidential election', *International Journal of Press/Politics*, 14(3): 335–52.

De la Torre, C. and E. Peruzzotti (2008) *El retorno del pueblo. Populismo y nuevas democracias en América Latina*, Quito: FLACSO/Ecuador and Ministry of Culture.

De Vengoechea, A. (2014) 'Clara López: la mujer rebelde', *El Tiempo*, Bogotá, 9 May, www.eltiempo.com/bocas/clara-lopez-en-entrevista-con-revista-bocas/13965202.

Deslauriers, J.-P. (2004) *Investigación cualitativa*, Pereira: Editorial Papiro.

Deutsch, K. (1990) *Política y gobierno: como el pueblo decide su destino*, Mexico: Fondo de Cultura Económica.

DeYoung, K., C. J. Duque and J. Forero (2011) 'La ayuda estadounidense, implicada en abusos de poder en Colombia', *Equipo Nizkor*, www.derechos.org/nizkor/ colombia/doc/usacol26.html.

Diamint, R. and L. Tedesco (eds) (2013) *Democratizar a los políticos. Un estudio sobre líderes latinoamericanos*, Madrid: Libros de la Catarata.

—— (2014) 'El liderazgo político sudamericano en perspectiva comparada', *Nueva Sociedad*, 249: 34–48.

Diamond, L., J. Linz and S. Lipset (1999) *Democracy in Developing Countries: Latin America*, Boulder, CO: Lynne Rienner.

Diamond, L., M. Plattner and D. Abente Brun (2008) *Latin America's Struggle for Democracy*, Baltimore, MD: Johns Hopkins University Press.

Durán Escalante, M. C. (2006) 'La reforma política de 2003: ¿más de lo mismo?', *Revista Javeriana*, 2(1): 113–35.

Economist (2013) 'The Economist's country of the year. Earth's got talent', 21 December, www.economist.com/news/leaders/21591872-resilient-ireland-booming-south-sudan-tumultuous-turkey-our-country-year-earths-got.

Economist Intelligence Unit (2013) *Democracy Index. Democracy in Retreat*, Economist Intelligent Unit, graphics.eiu.com/PDF/Democracy_Index_2010_web.pdf.

Edwards, S. (2009) *Populismo o Mercado*, Buenos Aires: Grupo Editorial Norma.

El Comercio (2013) 4 January, 6.

El Espectador (2014) 'El Uruguay de Mujica tras cuatro años de gestión del mandatario', Bogotá, 22 October, www.elespectador.com/noticias/elmundo/el-uruguay-de-mujica-tras-cuatro-anos-de-gestion-del-ma-articulo-523496.

El Nuevo Herald (2014) 'Acusan a ex presidente colombiano Álvaro Uribe de presuntos nexos con narcos y paramilitares', www.elnuevoherald.com/noticias/mundo/america-latina/colombia-es/article2144148.html.

El País (1989) 2 December.

—— (2009) 'El presidente guerrillero', 6 December, elpais.com/diario/2009/12/06/domingo/1260075160_850215.html.

—— (2014) 'Las presidenciales de Uruguay marcan un hito de juego limpio', 1 December, internacional.elpais.com/internacional/2014/12/01/actualidad/1417400455_910304.html.

El Tiempo (2000) 'Pastrana debe exigir respeto a las FARC: SIP', 15 March, www.eltiempo.com/archivo/documento/MAM-1277810.

—— (2014) 'Iván Cepeda acusa de graves delitos a Álvaro Uribe en su último libro', www.eltiempo.com/archivo/documento/CMS-13577835.

El Universo (2005) 14 October, 8.

Ellner, S. (1988) *Venezuela's Movimiento Al Socialismo: From Guerrilla Defeat to Innovative Politics*, Durham, NC: Duke University Press.

Elo, S. and H. Kyngäs (2008) 'The qualitative content analysis process', *Journal of Advanced Nursing*, 62(1): 107–15.

Elster, J. (2010) *La explicación del comportamiento social. Más tuercas y tornillos para las ciencias sociales*, Buenos Aires: Editorial Gedisa.

Encuesta a Diputados Argentinos (2003–07), americo.usal.es/oir/Elites/eliteca.htm.

Erez, M. and E. Gati (2004) 'A dynamic, multi-level model of culture: from the micro level of the individual to the macro-level of a global culture', *Applied Psychology: An International Review*, 53(4): 583–98.

Estudios Económicos de la OCDE (2013) *Colombia, Evaluación económica*, oecd.org/eco/surveys/Colombia_Overview_ESP%20NEW.pdf.

Fabbrini, S. (2009) *El ascenso del Príncipe democrático*, Buenos Aires: Fondo de Cultura Económica.

Fidanza, E. (2009) 'Decálogo de la anomia argentina', *La Nación*, 19 November, www.lanacion.com.ar.

—— (2010) 'Las paradojas de Argentina', *La Nación*, 4 June, www.lanacion.com.ar.

Fiol, C. Marlene et al. (1999) 'Charismatic leadership: strategies for effecting social change', *Leadership Quarterly*, 10(3): 449–82.

Flick, U. (2012) *Introducción a la investigación cualitativa*, Madrid: Ediciones Morata and Fundación Paideia Galiza.

FM Centro (2015) '"Pepe" Mujica donó 550 mil dólares de su sueldo para viviendas', 10 January, fmcentrobasavilbaso.com/-quotpepe-quot-mujica-don-550-mil-dolares-de-su-sueldo-para-viviendas_n-15521.htm.

Freidenberg, F. (2008) '¿Renovación o continuismo? Actitudes, valores y trayectoria de la clase política ecuatoriana', *Ecuador Debate*, 75: 131–46.

Fukuyama, F. (2008) 'Do defective institutions explain the development gap between the United States and Latin America?', in F. Fukuyama (ed.), *Falling Behind. Explaining the development gap between Latin America and the United States*, Oxford: Oxford University Press.

—— (2012) 'The future of history: can liberal democracy survive the decline of the middle class', *Foreign Affairs*, 91(53): 53–61.

—— (2013) 'What is governance', Working Paper 314, Center for Global Development, www.cgdev.org/publication/what-governance-working-paper-314.

Galindo Hernández, C. (2007) 'Neopopulismo en Colombia: el caso del gobierno de Álvaro Uribe Vélez', *Iconos. Revista de Ciencias Sociales*, 27: 147–62.

Garcé, A. (2009) *El giro republicano. Bases conceptuales del déficit democrático de América Latina*, Montevideo: Ediciones Trilce.

—— (2010) 'Uruguay 2009: de Tabaré Vázquez a José Mujica', *Revista de Ciencia Política*, 30(2): 499–535.

García Martín, M. (2009) 'Jóvenes políticos parlamentarios', *Boletín Datos de Opinión*, Elites Parlamentarias Latinoamericanas, americo.usal.es/oir/Elites/Boletines%204/6_García.pdf.

Garea, F. (2010) 'Los diputados son libres, sus votos no', *El País*, 30 June, www.elpais.es.

Geddes, B. (1994) *Politician's Dilemma. Building state capacity in Latin America*, Berkeley, CA: University of California Press.

Germani, G. (1965) *Política y sociedad en una época de transición*, Buenos Aires: Paidós.

—— (1971) *Sociología de la Modernización*, Buenos Aires: Paidós.

Gerring, J. (2008) *Social Science Methodology. A Critical Framework*, New York: Cambridge University Press.

González, L. (1985) 'El sistema de partidos y las perspectivas de la democracia uruguaya', *Revista Mexicana de Sociología*, 47(2): 67–84.

Habermas, J. (2006) 'Political communication in media society: does democracy still enjoy an epistemic dimension? The impact of normative theory on empirical research', *Communication Theory*, 16(4): 411–26.

Hagopian, F. (2005) 'Derechos, representación y la creciente calidad de la democracia en Brasil y Chile', *Política y Gobierno*, 12(1): 41–90.

Harvard Business School (2011) *On Leadership*, Cambridge, MA: Harvard Business School.

Held, D. (1996) *Models of Democracy*, Cambridge: Polity Press.

Helms, L. (2012) *Comparative Political Leadership*, Basingstoke: Palgrave Macmillan.

Hermann, M. G. and J. D. Hagan (2001) 'International decision making: leadership matters', in K. Mingst and J. Snider, *Essential Readings in World Politics*, New York and London: The Norton Series in World Politics.

Hirschman, A. (1970) *Exit, Voice, and Loyalty: Responses to Decline in Firms, Organizations, and States*, Cambridge, MA: Harvard University Press.

House, R. et al. (1991) 'Personality and charisma in the US presidency: a psychological theory of leader effectiveness', *Administrative Science Quarterly*, 36(3): 364–96.

Hurtado, O. (2006) *Los costos del populismo*, Quito: CORDES.

—— (2007) *El poder político en el Ecuador*, Quito: Planeta.

—— (2010) 'Know thyself. Latin America in the mirror of culture', *The American Interest*, January/February, 92–102.

Ibáñez, A. M. and J. C. Muñoz (2011) 'La persistencia de la concentración de la tierra en Colombia. ¿Qué pasó entre 2000 y 2010?', *Notas de Política*, 9, p. 3.

Jones, M. (2008) 'The recruitment and selection of legislative candidates in Argentina', in P. Siavelis and S. Morgenstern (eds), *Path to Power. Political recruitment and candidate selection in Latin America*, Pennsylvania: Pennsylvania University Press, pp. 41–75.

Jones, M. et al. (2002) 'Amateur legislators – professional politicians: the consequences of party-centered electoral rules in a federal system', *American Journal of Political Science*, 46(3): 656–69.

Kane, J. and H. Patapan (2012) *The Democratic Leader: How Democracy Defines, Empowers and Limits Its Leaders*, Oxford: Oxford University Press.

Karl, T. L. (1986) 'Petroleum and political pacts: the transition to democracy in Venezuela', in G. O'Donnell, P. Schmitter and L. Whitehead (eds), *Transitions from Authoritarian Rule. Latin America*, Baltimore, MD: Johns Hopkins University Press.

—— (1995) 'The Venezuelan petro-state and the crisis of "its" democracy', in J. McCoy et al. (eds), *Venezuelan Democracy under Stress*, New Brunswick, NJ: Transaction Press.

—— (2004) 'Latin America. Virtuous or perverse cycle', in G. O'Donnell, J. Vargas Cullell and O. Iazzetta, *The Quality of Democracy. Theory and applications*, Indiana: University of Notre Dame Press.

Kellerman, B. (2004) *Bad Leadership*, Cambridge, MA: Harvard Business School Press.

—— (2012) *The End of Leadership*, Cambridge, MA: Harvard Business School Press.

Klein, K. and R. House (1995) 'On fire: charismatic leadership and level of analysis', *Leadership Quarterly*, 6(2): 183–98.

La Vanguardia (2011) Informe de Desarrollo Humano Colombia 2011 del PNUD, 'Colombia, uno de los países más desiguales por alta concentración de tierras', 25 September, Barcelona, www.vanguardia.com/actualidad/colombia/123785-colombia-uno-de-los-paises-mas-desiguales-por-alta-concentracion-de-tierras.

Lagos, M. (2006) 'A apearse de la fantasía: Hugo Chávez y los liderazgos en América Latina', *Nueva Sociedad*, 205: 92–101.

Lanzaro, J. (2001) 'Uruguay: las alternativas de un presidencialismo pluralista', in J. Lanzaro (ed.), *Tipos de presidencialismo y coaliciones políticas en América Latina*, Buenos Aires: CLACSO, pp. 283–307.

Lanzaro, J. and G. de Armas (2012) 'Uruguay: clases medias y procesos electorales en una democracia de partidos', Working Paper 04/12, Montevideo: Instituto de Ciencia Política, Universidad de la República.

Larrea, T. (2007) *¿En qué pensamos los ecuatorianos al hablar de democracia?*, Quito: Corporación Participación Ciudadana.

Latinobarómetro (2013) *Informe Latinobarómetro 2013*, www.latinobarometro. org/latContents.jsp.

Leal, D. and D. Roll (2013) 'Tanques de pensamiento y partidos políticos en Colombia. El caso de las reformas políticas de 2003 y 2009', *Ciencia Política*, 16: 100.

Levitsky, S. and M. V. Murillo (2008) 'Argentina: from Kirchner to Kirchner', in L. Diamond, M. Plattner and D. Abente Brun (eds), *Latin America's Struggle for Democracy*, Baltimore, MD: Johns Hopkins University Press.

Levitsky, S. and K. Roberts (eds) (2011) *Latin America's Left Turn: Causes and Implications*, Baltimore, MD: Johns Hopkins University Press.

Levy Yeyati, E. and M. Novaro (2013) *Vamos por todo*, Buenos Aires: Editorial Sudamericana.

Linz, J. (1990) 'The perils of presidentialism', *Journal of Democracy*, 1(1): 51–69.

Linz, J. and A. Valenzuela (1994) *The Failure of Presidential Democracies*, Baltimore, MD: Johns Hopkins University Press.

Lodola, G. (2009) 'La estructura subnacional de las carreras políticas en Argentina y Brasil', *Desarrollo Económico*, 49(194): 247–86.

López Buenaño, F. (2010) 'Embuste, manipulación y realismo mágico en el liderazgo político', *Polemika, Revista Cuatrimestral del Instituto de Economía*, Universidad San Francisco de Quito, 1(3): 48–62.

López Estrada, R. E. and J.-P. Deslauriers (2011) 'La entrevista cualitativa como técnica para la investigación en Trabajo Social', *Margen*, 61: 1–19.

López Pacheco, J. A. (2012) 'Las organizaciones no gubernamentales de derechos humanos en la democracia. Aproximaciones para el estudio de la politización de los derechos humanos en Colombia', *Estudios Políticos*, 41: 103–23.

Lord, C. (2003) *The Modern Prince: What Leaders Need to Know Now*, New Haven, CT, and London: Yale University Press.

Lukes, S. (2005) *Power: A Radical View*, 2nd edn, London: Palgrave.

Luna, J. P. (2007) 'Frente Amplio and the crafting of a social democratic alternative in Uruguay', *Latin American Politics and Society*, 49(4): 1–30.

Magdaleno, J. (2013) 'La historia de un desencanto: el fin de la democracia pactada y el ascenso de la Revolución Chavista en Venezuela', in R. Diamint and L. Tedesco (eds), *Democratizar a los políticos. Un estudio sobre líderes latinoamericanos*, Madrid: Libros de la Catarata.

Mahoney, J., E. Kimball and K. Koivu (2009) 'The logic of historical explanation in the social sciences', *Comparative Political Studies*, 42(1): 114–46.

Mainwaring, S. (2008) 'The crisis of representation in the Andes', in L. Diamond, M. Plattner and D. Abente Brun (eds), *Latin America's Struggle for Democracy*, Baltimore, MD: Johns Hopkins University Press.

Mainwaring, S. and T. R. Scully (eds) (1995) *Building Democratic Institutions: Party Systems in Latin America*, Stanford, CA: Stanford University Press.

—— (2010) *Democratic Governance in Latin America*, Stanford, CA: Stanford University Press.

Malamud, C. (2010) *Populismos latinoamericanos*, Madrid: Ediciones Nobel.

Mandujano Bustamante, F. (1998) 'Teoría del muestreo: particularidades del diseño muestral en estudios de la conducta social', *Revista Electrónica de Metodología Aplicada*, 3(1): 1–15.

Marcano, C. and A. Barrera (2007) *Hugo Chávez: The Definitive Biography of Venezuela's Controversial President*, New York: Random House.

Masciulli, J., M. A. Molchanov and A. Knight (2009) *Political Leadership in Context*, The Ashgate Research Companion to Political Leadership, Surrey: Ashgate and Gower eBooks, www.ashgate.com/pdf/SamplePages/Ashgate_Research_Companion_to_Political_Leadership_Intro.pdf.

Mayorga, R. (2006) 'Outsiders and neopopulism: the road to plesbiscitary democracy', in S. Mainwairing, A. M. Bejarano and E. Pizarro (eds) *The Crisis of Democratic Representation in the Andes*, Stanford, CA: Stanford University Press.

McCoy, J. L. (1999) 'Chavez and the end of "partyarchy" in Venezuela', *Journal of Democracy*, 10(3): 64–77.

Meindl, J., S. Ehrlich and J. Dukerich (1985) 'The romance of leadership', *Administrative Science Quarterly*, 30(1): 78–102.

Mejía Quintana, Ó. (2009) 'Un análisis penetrante y descarnado de la cultura política bajo Uribe y bajo las FARC, y de su intenso contraste con los valores de la Constitución de 1991', *Razón Pública*, 26 October, www.razonpublica.com/index.php/qu%C3%A9-es-raz%C3%B3n-p%C3%BAblica.html.

Michels, R. (1962) *Political Parties*, New York: Crowell-Collier.

Miliband, R. (1969) *The State in Capitalist Society*, London: Weidenfeld & Nicolson.

Ministerio de Coordinación de Desarrollo Social de Ecuador (n.d.) www.desarrollosocial.gob.ec/.

Monaldi, F., R. Obuchi and A. Guerra (2010) 'Las elecciones legislativas de 2010 en Venezuela: cuando dos más dos no son cuatro', *Temas de Coyuntura*, 62: 37–77.

Montúfar, C. (2008) 'El populismo intermitente de Lucio Gutiérrez', in C. de la Torre and E. Peruzzotti, *El retorno del pueblo. Populismo y nuevas democracias en América Latina*, Quito: FLACSO.

Morales, A. (1978) 'Colombia: elecciones y crisis política', *Nueva Sociedad*, 34: 59–61.

Moreira, C. (2008) 'Problematizando la historia de Uruguay: un análisis de las relaciones entre el estado, la política y sus protagonistas', in M. López Maya, N. Íñigo Carrera and P. Calveiro (eds), *Luchas contrahegemónicas y cambios políticos recientes en América Latina*, Buenos Aires: CLACSO, 365–81.

Morlino, L. (1991) 'Problemas y opciones en la Comparación', in G. Sartori and L. Morlino (eds), *La Comparación en ciencias sociales*, Madrid: Alianza Editorial.

Muñoz, H. (2008) *La sombra del dictador*, Barcelona: Paidós.

Navia, P. and I. Walker (2010) 'Political institutions, populism, and democracy in Latin America', in S. Mainwaring and T. Scully, *Democratic Governance in Latin America*, Stanford, CA: Stanford University Press.

Nolan, R. (2012) 'The realest reality show in the world', *New York Times*, May, www.nytimes.com/2012/05/06/magazine/hugo-chavezs-totally-bizarre-talk-show.html?pagewanted=1.

Norris, P. (2004) 'Who surfs? New technology, old voters and virtual democracy in US elections 1992–2000', Shorenstein Center on the Press, Politics and Public Policy, John F. Kennedy School of Government, Harvard University, www.hks.harvard.edu/fs/pnorris/Acrobat/WhoSurfs%20Revised%202001.pdf.

—— (2011) *Democratic Deficit. Critical Citizens Revisited*, Cambridge: Cambridge University Press.

Nun, J. (2000) *Democracia. ¿Gobierno del pueblo o de los políticos?*, Buenos Aires: Fondo de Cultura Económica.

Nye, J. (2008) *The Powers to Lead*, Oxford: Oxford University Press.

O'Donnell, G. (1995) 'Delegative democracy', *Journal of Democracy*, 5(1): 55–69.

—— (2004) 'Human development, human rights and democracy', in G. O'Donnell, J. Vargas Cullell and O. Iazzetta (eds), *The Quality of democracy. Theory and applications*, Indiana: University of Notre Dame Press.

O'Donnell, G., J. Vargas Cullell and O. Iazzetta (2004) *The Quality of Democracy. Theory and Applications*, Indiana: University of Notre Dame Press.

Obama, B. (2007) *The Audacity of Hope*, New York: Canongate.

OEA and PNUD (2009) *La democracia de ciudadanía*, www.democraciadeciu-dadania.org/agenda.html.

Ogliastri, E. et al. (1999) 'Cultura y liderazgo organizacional en 10 países de América Latina: el estudio GLOBE', *Academia, Revista Latinoamericana de Administración*, 22: 29–57.

Ollier, M. M. (2001) *Las coaliciones políticas en la Argentina. El caso de la Alianza*, Buenos Aires: Fondo de Cultura Económica.

—— (2008) 'La institucionalización democrática en el callejón: la inestabilidad presidencial argentina (1999–2003)', *América Latina Hoy*, 49: 73–103.

—— (2013) 'La democracia invertida: entre la abdicación y la dominación. Hacia su formación conceptual en un estudio de caso', in R. Diamint and L. Tedesco (eds), *Democratizar a los políticos. Un estudio sobre líderes latinoamericanos*, Madrid: Libros de la Catarata.

Ortiz, A. (2008) 'Populismo y transnacionalidad. Una hipótesis sobre el liderazgo de Chávez y Correa', *Ecuador Debate*, 73: 63–76.

Ospina Peralta, P. (2006) 'La crisis del clientelismo en Ecuador', *Ecuador Debate*, 69: 57–76.

Página 12 (2010) 'Asume Mujica un nuevo liderazgo en Uruguay', 1 March, www.pagina12.com.ar/diario/elmundo/4-141179-2010-03-01.html.

Panizza, F. (ed.) (2005) *Populism and the Mirror of Democracy*, London: Verso.

Pastrana, A. (n.d.) 'Algunas reflexiones sobre la libertad de prensa', www.andrespastrana.org/biblioteca/algunas-reflexiones-sobre-la-libertad-de-prensa/.

Patton, M. Q. (1990) *Qualitative Evaluation Methods*, Beverly Hills, CA: Sage.

Pérez Liñán, A. (2007) 'El método comparativo: fundamentos y desarrollos recientes', Working paper, Pittsburgh University, www.pitt.edu/~asp27/USAL/2007.Fundamentos.pdf.

—— (2009) *Juicio político al presidente y nueva inestabilidad política en América Latina*, Buenos Aires: Fondo de Cultura Económica.

Peters, G. (1998) *Comparative Politics, Theory and Method*, New York: New York University Press.

Philip, G. and F. Panizza (2011) *The Triumph of Politics*, Cambridge: Polity Press.

Pizarro Leongómez, E. (1996) 'La crisis de los partidos y los partidos en crisis', in F. Leal Buitrago (ed.) *Tras la huella de la crisis política*, Bogotá: Tercer Mundo-IEPRI-FESCOL, pp. 218–19.

Pla, M. (1999) 'El rigor en la investigación cualitativa', *Atención Primaria*, Barcelona, 24(5): 295–300.

Presidencia de la República (2013) 'Palabras del Presidente Juan Manuel Santos al intervenir en el Foro Nacional sobre Libertad de Prensa en Colombia', wsp.presidencia.gov.co/Prensa/2013/Mayo/Paginas/20130514_05.aspx.

Przewroski, A. and C. Curvale (2008) 'Does politics explain the economic gap between the United States and Latin America?', in F. Fukuyama (ed.), *Falling Behind. Explaining the development gap between Latin America and the United States*, Oxford: Oxford University Press.

Quiroga, H. (2010) *La República desolada. Los cambios políticos de la Argentina (2001–2009)*, Buenos Aires: Edhasa.

Ramírez Huertas, G. (2009) 'Fragmentación partidista en Colombia', *Estudios en Derecho y Gobierno*, 2(1).

Reid, M. (2007) *Forgotten Continent. The Battle for Latin America's Soul*, New Haven, CT, and London: Yale University Press.

Restrepo, L. A. (2006) 'Hacia el reino de los caudillos ilustrados. Los gobiernos colombianos como actores políticos', in F. Leal Buitrago (ed.), *En la encrucijada: Colombia en el siglo XXI*, Bogotá: Grupo Editorial Norma, 27–49.

Rey, J. C. (1998) *El futuro de la democracia en Venezuela*, Caracas: Ediciones de la Facultad de Ciencias Jurídicas y Políticas, Universidad Central de Venezuela.

Rial, J. (1990) 'Los partidos políticos uruguayos en el proceso de transición hacia la democracia', Working Paper 145, Notre Dame, IN: Kellogg Institute.

Richard, E. (n.d.) 'Álvaro Uribe: la comunicación por la imagen. Principios de marketing político', *Opera. Observatorio de Política Ejecución y Resultados de la Administración Pública*, 8: 73.

Rilla, J. (1999) 'Cambiar la historia. Historia política y elite política en el Uruguay contemporáneo', *Revista Uruguaya de Ciencia Política*, 11: 107–27.

—— (2008) 'Uruguay 1985–2007: restauración, reforma, crisis y cambio electoral', *Revista Nuestra América*, 6: 63–95.

Roberts, K. M. (2003) 'Party system demise and populist resurgence in Venezuela', *Latin American Politics and Society*, 45(3): 35–57.

—— (2008) 'El resurgimiento del populismo latinoamericano', in C. de la Torre and E. Peruzzotti (eds), *El retorno del pueblo. Populismo y nuevas democracias en América Latina*, Quito: FLACSO/Ecuador and Ministry of Culture.

Rodríguez, J. M. (2010) 'El fenómeno de la levadura', *Polemika, Revista Cuatrimestral del Instituto de Economía*, 1(3): 3–7.

Rodríguez Garavito, C. A. (2005) 'El impacto de la reelección sobre la política y las instituciones colombianas', *Revista Foro, Revista de Ciencias Jurídicas y Sociales*, 56: 14.

Rodríguez Raga, J. C. and M. A. Seligson (eds) (2012) *Cultura política de la democracia en Colombia y en las Américas, 2012: Hacia la igualdad de oportunidades*, Nashville, TN: Vanderbilt University.

Rodríguez Rincón, Y. (2006) 'La reelección presidencial inmediata y el movimiento de la democracia en Colombia', *Análisis Político*, 58: 79–80.

Roll, D. (2001) *Un siglo de ambigüedad. Para entender cien años de crisis y reformas políticas en Colombia*, Bogotá: IEPRI, CEREC and Facultad de Derecho, Ciencias Políticas y Sociales, Universidad Nacional de Colombia.

—— (2002) *Rojo difuso y azul pálido. Los partidos tradicionales en Colombia: entre el debilitamiento y la persistencia*, Bogotá: Facultad de Derecho, Ciencias Políticas y Sociales, Universidad Nacional de Colombia.

Romero, A. (1996) *La miseria del populismo*, Caracas: Editorial Panapo.

Rosenzweig, P. (2007) 'The halo effect, and other managerial delusions', *McKinsey Quarterly*, 1: 77–85.

Salgado, J. (1990) 'La práctica del muestreo', in E. Ortega Martínez (ed.), *Manual de investigación comercial*, Madrid: Pirámide, 344–77.

Sartori, G. (1991) 'Comparación y método comparativo', in G. Sartori and L. Morlino (eds), *La Comparación en ciencias sociales*, Madrid: Alianza Editorial.

Semana (2011) 'Constitución de 1991: inclusión política vs. exclusión social', Bogotá, 7 February, www.semana.com/opinion/expertos/articulo/constitucion-1991-inclusion-politica-vs-exclusion-social/322655.

—— (2014) '¿Quiénes son esta vez?', Bogotá, 1 March, www.semana.com/confidenciales/articulo/descendientes-de-las-famosas-ibanez/379110-3.

Serna, M. (2005) 'Las vías hacia el poder político. Bases sociales y carreras parlamentarias', in E. Mazzei (ed.), *El Uruguay desde la Sociología IV*, Montevideo: Departamento de Sociología, Universidad de la República, 9–30.

—— (2009) 'La composición de la elite política uruguaya: circulación y reconversión en democracia', Paper presented at the XXI World Congress of Political Science, IPSA, Santiago, 1–20.

Shamir, B. et al. (1993) 'The motivational effects of charismatic leadership: a self-concept based theory', *Organization Science*, 4(4): 577–94.

Smulovitz, C. and E. Peruzzotti (2000) 'Societal accountability in Latin America', *Journal of Democracy*, 11(4): 147–58.

Szwarcberg, M. (2012) 'Actos partidarios y clientelismo político en América Latina', *Nueva Sociedad*, 240: 110–18.

Tanaka, M. (2013) 'Liderazgos y crisis de representación partidaria: ¿cuándo son una variable política relevante? Una aproximación desde los países andinos', in R. Diamint and L. Tedesco (eds), *Democratizar a los políticos. Un estudio sobre líderes latinoamericanos*, Madrid: Libros de la Catarata.

Taylor, S. J. and R. Bogdan (1987) *Introducción a los métodos cualitativos de investigación*, Buenos Aires: Paidós.

Tedesco, L. (2002) 'Argentina's turmoil: the politics of informality and the roots of economic meltdown', *Cambridge Review of International Affairs*, 15(3): 469–81.

Tedesco, L. and R. Diamint (eds) (2013) 'Fallas de liderazgo político en perspectiva comparada', in *Democratizar a los políticos. Un estudio sobre líderes latinoamericanos*, Madrid: Libros de la Catarata.

Teles, F. (2012) 'Political leaders: the paradox of freedom and democracy', *Revista Enfoques, Ciencia Política y Administración Pública*, X(16): 112–31.

—— (2013) 'The distinctiveness of democratic political leadership', *Political Studies Review*, 12(2): 1–15.

Thorndike, E. (1920a) 'Intelligence and its uses', *Harper's Monthly*, January, pp. 227–35.

—— (1920b) 'A constant error in psychological ratings', *Journal of Applied Psychology*, 4(1): 25–9.

Tickner, A. B. (2003) 'Convergencias y contradicciones en las políticas internas y externas de Colombia: de Andrés Pastrana a Álvaro Uribe', Paper presented at the Latin American Studies Association (LASA), Dallas, Texas, 27–29 March, lasa.international.pitt.edu/Lasa2003/TicknerArlene.pdf.

Trinkunas, H. A. (2002) 'The crisis in Venezuelan civil–military relations: from Punto Fijo to the Fifth Republic', *Latin American Research Review*, 37(1): 41–76.

Tucker, R. (1977) 'Personality and political leadership', *Political Science Quarterly*, 92(3): 383–93.

Urrego Ardila, M. Á. (2013) 'El movimiento sindical, el período de la violencia y la formación de la nueva izquierda colombiana, 1959–1971', *Diálogo de Saberes*, 38: 135–45.

Valenzuela, A. (2004) 'Latin American presidencies interrupted', *Journal of Democracy*, 15(4): 5–19.

Van Cott, D. (2008) *Radical Democracy in the Andes*, Cambridge: Cambridge University Press.

Viteri Díaz, G. (2006) 'Situación de la educación en el Ecuador', *Observatorio de la Economía Latinoamericana*, 70, www.eumed.net/cursecon/ecolat/index.htm.

Waldman, D. et al. (2001) 'Does leadership matter? CEO leadership attributes and profitability under conditions of perceived environmental uncertainty', *Academy of Management Journal*, 44(1): 134–43.

Webb, P., T. Poguntke and R. Kolodny (2012) 'The presidentialization of party leadership? Evaluating party leadership and party government in the democratic world', in L. Helms (ed.), *Comparative Political Leadership*, Basingstoke: Palgrave Macmillan.

Weber, M. (1984) *Economía y Sociedad*, 7th edn, Mexico: Fondo de Cultura Económica.

Youngs, R. (2015) *The Puzzle of Non-Western Democracy*, Washington, DC: Carnegie Endowment for International Peace.

Index